The Art of
PAPER CRAFTS

Compiled by Jilly MacLeod

SMITHMARK

© Salamander Books Ltd, 1991
129-137 York Way,
London N7 9LG,
United Kingdom

ISBN 0-8317-0435-7

This edition published in 1991 by SMITHMARK Publishers Inc.,
16 East 32nd Street, New York, NY 10016.

SMITHMARK books are available for bulk purchase for sales
promotion and premium use. For details write or telephone
the Manager of Special Sales, SMITHMARK Publishers Inc.,
16 East 32nd Street , New York, NY 10016. (212) 532-6600.

CREDITS

Craft Designs by: Cheryl Owen, Rosalind Burdett, Annette Claxton,
Suzie Major, Susy Smith and Juliet Bawden
Editor-in-chief: Jilly Glassborow
Designers: Kathy Gummer, Philip Gorton and Tony Truscott
Photographers: Steve Tanner and Terry Dilliway
Typeset by: Barbican Print and Marketing Services, London, and the Old Mill, London
Color Separation by: Fotographics Ltd, London – Hong Kong and Scantrans Pte Ltd., Singapore
Printed in Italy

CONTENTS

PAPER CRAFTS FOR THE HOME

INTRODUCTION

Paper is a remarkably versatile material and rather
underated as a durable and exciting craft medium. It is available
in a wide range of types, from flimsy gossamer tissue to tough, practical
cardboard, from simple gummed squares to exquisite gift wraps. You will probably have
a number of materials already to hand at home; but virtually all the items
mentioned in this book are easy to obtain from stationers, craft shops
and art suppliers, and are relatively inexpensive to buy.

In Section One of *The Art of Paper Crafts* we will show
you how to transform paper and cardboard into a vast array of both
decorative and practical items for the home. We have included original gift
ideas such as pictures, picture frames, lampshades, letter racks, and personalized
stationery. There is also a chapter devoted to children's designs, where
you will find ideas to brighten up kids' bedrooms, as well as
projects which children can undertake themselves. A host of
festive garlands, party pieces, table decorations
and place settings complete the section.

I f you look around your home you may be surprised to find how many suitable materials you already have from which to make your designs – materials such as left-over wrapping paper and wallpaper, or cardboard packets and boxes that can be cut up and re-used.

PAPER

The range of papers available for paper crafts is endless and very inspiring. Apart from plain coloured papers available from art and craft shops, there is a wide variety of handmade papers and exotic gift wraps that will add a touch of sophistication to any design. Textured and flock papers are also available, adding a third dimension to collages.

Crepe paper is a very adaptable material because it stretches and comes in a wide range of colours. When cut against the grain, the cut edge can be gently stretched to give an attractive fluted edge.

Tissue paper and iridescent film, although delicate, can be used to stunning effect on mobiles or as a lining for handmade boxes and bowls. Paper doilies and pictures from greeting cards or magazines are perfect for making gift tags and greeting cards or to decorate boxes.

Brightly coloured gummed paper squares are easy to apply – you simply moisten the back and stick in position. This type of paper is very convenient when working on an intricate design.

CARDBOARD

Generally, where cardboard is required for a project, you should use thin, lightweight cardboard, roughly the same thickness as that used for cereal packets. Where thick cardboard has been suggested, it should be sturdy enough to crease when bent. Some cardboards have a thin coating on one side which has an attractive shiny, metallic or textured

finish. These are particularly good for making party hats and masks. Mounting board can be used for items that will be handled a lot. It is made up of layers of cardboard and comes in many thicknesses.

CRAFT ACCESSORIES

Even though you may wish to specialize in paper crafts, this shouldn't exclude using a wide range of other materials in conjunction with paper for that extra special effect. It is often the finishing touches that make a handmade item so special, and you will find craft shops are a treasure trove of suitable decorative objects – many of them very reasonably priced. Cotton pulp or polystyrene shapes are lightweight and suitable for decorating in many ways. Similarly, coloured pipecleaners, tiny pom-poms, stick on eyes, beads, sequins and jewellery components all add interest to a design.

Nowadays, there is an exciting range of Victorian scraps that are ideal for paper crafts, plus a wide variety of decorative sticky tapes that help give a professional finish to a project. Giftwrapping ribbons can also be used to great effect. They come in many colours and widths. The wide ribbons can be moistened so that they will stick to themselves and the narrow ribbons will coil attractively when pulled smoothly over the blade of a pair of scissors.

A wide range of different coloured and textured papers is available from art and craft shops, and the choice can be increased one hundred-fold if you also consider using wrapping paper or wallpaper for your designs. Giftwrapping ribbons, adhesive tapes, pipecleaners and pom-poms also come in a variety of bright colours and help add the finishing touches.

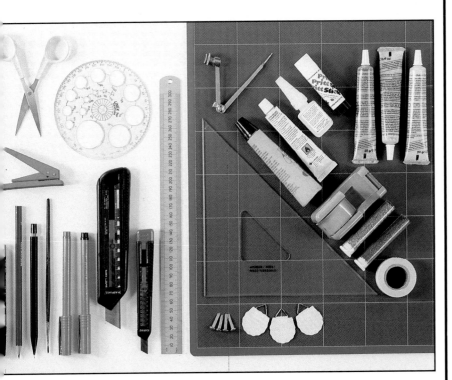

Here are just some of the things you will find useful when working with paper. They include a cutting mat, set square, steel rule, compass, craft knife and scissors, plus a range of pencils, pens, glues and tapes.

You may well find that you already have much of the basic equipment required for working with paper and cardboard at home. For best results, be sure to work on a clean, flat surface and, for safety, be sure not to leave any sharp implements lying around afterwards for children to find.

PENCILS AND DRAWING AIDS

An HB pencil is the most versatile pencil to use, but a softer lead such as 2B is better for sketching. Always keep pencils sharpened to a fine point so that your drawing is accurate. Be sure to use a ruler for drawing straight lines. A set square should be used for drawing squares and rectangles so that the angles are correct. Draw circles with a compass or, for tiny circles, use a plastic stencil.

SCISSORS AND KNIVES

A sharp, pointed pair of scissors is essential for working with paper. A small pair is more useful and easier to handle than a large pair. Craft knives give a better finish than scissors when cutting thick cardboard. Replace the blades frequently as they soon become blunt.

Always cut on a cutting mat – use a purpose-made mat or improvise, using a piece of corrugated cardboard. When cutting through thick cardboard, do not cut right through in one go but make several cuts, going deeper each time. Cut straight lines against a steel rule, preferably a safety one to protect your fingers. When cardboard needs to be folded, 'score' the surface lightly with a craft knife, being sure not to cut too deep into the board.

ADHESIVES AND TAPES

It is important to use the right glue for the job. Read the manufacturer's instructions carefully and test glues on scraps of paper first. When sticking thin papers together, make sure the glue does not seep through the paper. Also take care with printed papers as some glues will smudge the pattern. Use a plastic spreader or strip of cardboard to apply glue evenly over a flat surface.

For a professional finish use spray adhesive. Either put your work on newspaper spread over the work surface or place it inside a box to protect the surrounding area from spray. Spray an even film over the surface and then stick in place. The sprayed paper can be repositioned which is very useful, and any tacky areas can be cleaned up with lighter fuel. Always use an ozone-friendly spray adhesive and work in a well ventilated room.

PVA medium has many purposes. It is a non-toxic, white solution that does not stain, and is quite suitable for children to use. It can be used as a glue and to make papier-mâché. As it dries to a clear, glossy finish, it is also useful as a protective varnish.

Double-sided tape is sticky on both sides and provides a neater, cleaner alternative to glue. Clear sticky tape is very-functional but remember that it does yellow and become brittle with age. An alternative is an opaque tape sometimes called magic or invisible tape which is longer-lasting but does not adhere so well.

Masking tape is a low-tack tape which is handy for holding paper and cardboard in place while you are working, and it does not leave a mark.

Paper and cardboard can be quite tough and durable, so in this chapter we have included a number of clever ideas which make thoughtful and personal gifts for family and friends. Jewellery, personalized stationery and letter racks, pictures and picture frames, are just some of the many attractive items you can create. There is also a stylish lampshade, stunning Chinese lantern and a variety of designs to enhance ordinary trinket boxes. And this chapter also provides a selection of projects showing you how to create little novelty items such as gift cones and bon-bon baskets, ideal for dinner or party guests to take home with them.

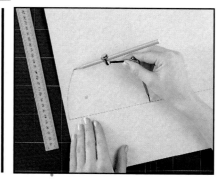

Fill this pretty cone with potpourri and allow the scent to waft through your home. Draw a 30cm (12in) diameter semi-circle with a compass on a piece of mottled peach-coloured paper. Cut it out and bend into the cone shape. Cut away a slice so the ends overlap smoothly and glue the overlapped ends together. Leave to dry.

Cut out motifs from a white paper doily and stick to the cone with spray glue. Coat the cone all over with PVA medium. Set aside until the medium has hardened and become clear and then apply two more coats.

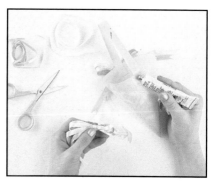

Cut a strip of paper 25cm x 1.5cm (10in x ⅝in) for the handle. Glue the ends inside the cone and coat with the PVA medium. Hang the handle over a door handle to dry. Tie ribbons in a bow and glue to the cone below the handle.

To make one of these pretty baskets you will need a sheet of paper 20cm (8in) square. Fold the square in half diagonally, then diagonally again. Place the triangle with the single fold running vertically. Bring the upper of the two free points up to meet the single point, opening the flap out as you do so to form a square. Crease the folds and repeat on the other side.

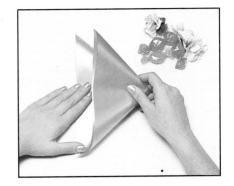

Position the newly formed square with the free edges pointing away from you. Fold the top free corner down to meet the opposite corner, then fold it back on itself to the horizontal centre line. Fold the flap in half once more. Repeat on the other side as shown. Turn the top left flap over to the right side, then fold it back on itself so that the corner meets the vertical centre line.

Fold the left hand corner in towards the vertical centre line also. Turn the basket over and repeat on the other side as shown. Open out the shape slightly and fold the top two flaps down inside the basket. Flatten the base. Cut a thin strip of paper for a handle and slip the ends into the slots on each side of the basket rim. Staple in place and decorate the basket with ribbons or lace.

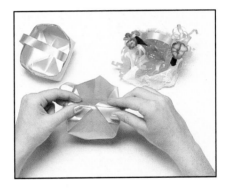

To make this simple gift for the table, fill a paper cone with chocolate drops or jellies for a children's party, or with sugared almonds for grown-ups. All you need is a small square of brightly coloured wrapping paper, a ribbon rosette, and some tissue paper. Simply roll the paper into a cone from corner to corner, taping it into a nice rounded shape.

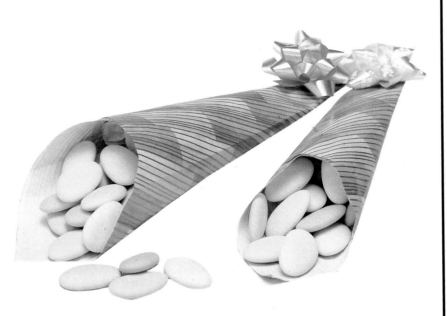

Flatten the cone slightly, positioning the top point in the centre; then fold up the bottom and stick on the ribbon rosette.

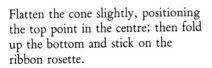

Scrunch up a little bit of tissue paper and slip it inside the cone to hold it in shape, then fill the top with sweets so that they spill out onto the point. You could attach a place card to each cone and use the cones to mark place settings at a large party.

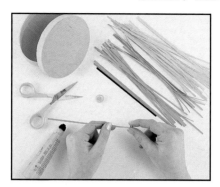

Quilling is the traditional papercraft of making pictures from coiled paper strips. Cut coloured paper strips 4mm (^{3}/$_{16}$in) wide and about 20cm (8in) long. Scratch the end of a strip to soften the paper. Now coil the strip tightly between your thumb and finger. Release the coil so it springs open and glue the end against one side.

The coils can be gently squeezed into various shapes to fit your chosen design. Experiment with forming different shapes such as triangles and teardrops. To make smaller coils, cut shorter paper strips.

Draw a design on the lid of a wooden box and spread paper glue on a section of the lid. Arrange the coils on the glue and then move onto the next section. Fill in the whole design – any gaps around the motif can be filled with coils that match the colour of the box.

Transform ordinary pencils into these smart covered ones with scraps of wrapping paper. Choose round rather than hexagonal-shaped pencils. Cut a strip of wrapping paper wide enough to wrap around the pencil and as long as the pencil. Spray the back heavily with spray glue and wrap around the pencil.

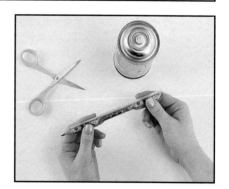

To finish, simply trim away the excess at the end of the pencil with a pair of small scissors.

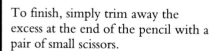

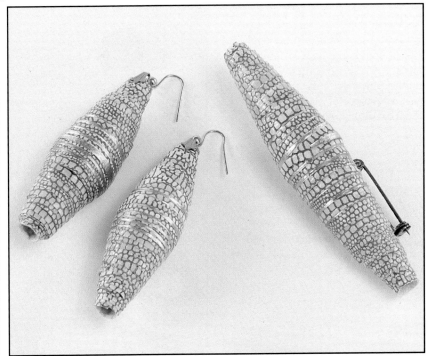

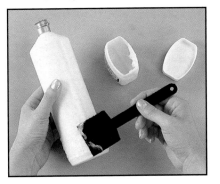

This bangle and matching necklace are made from papier-mâché. You will need suitable moulds for each – a small washing-up liquid bottle is the right size for the bangle and a garden stick is ideal for the beads. Cover the stick and 5cm (2in) at the end of the bottle with Vaseline. This stops the papier-mâché sticking to the mould.

Tear paper into small strips. Wallpaper lining paper was used for the bangle and newspaper for the necklace. Mix PVA medium (available at art shops) with a little water to thin it. Dip a brush in the solution, pick up a strip with the brush and press it onto the mould. Cover the Vaseline overlapping the strips. Apply four layers and leave to dry.

Build up the layers to about 5mm (¼in) thick and allow to dry overnight. Remove the jewellery, trim the bangle to 3cm (1¼in) wide with a craft knife and cut beads 3cm (1¼in) long. Tear giftwrap into small strips and apply to jewellery with the thinned PVA solution. Apply two coats of PVA medium as varnish. Thread beads onto cord.

No one will guess that this beautiful jewellery is made of paper. For each earring cut a long triangle of snakeskin-effect paper (available from specialist art shops) 76cm (30in) long with a 6cm (2¼in) wide base and gold giftwrap 75cm (29in) long with a 5cm (2in) wide base. Using PVA medium stick the giftwrap centrally to the wide end of the snakeskin piece.

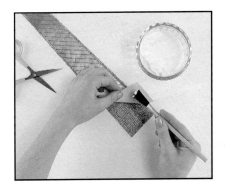

Spread Vaseline on a length of wood dowel to stop the paper sticking to the wood. Starting at the wide end, roll the triangles tightly around the dowel, brushing with PVA medium as you go. Give the beads a final coat of the medium as a varnish, leave to dry, then gently remove the dowel.

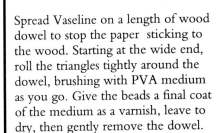

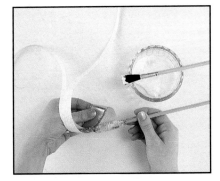

Pierce a hole through the top of each earring and attach a triangle wire. Fix a small jump ring to the triangle wire with a pair of pliers. Attach an earring hook to the ring. The brooch is made in the same way with wider triangles of snakeskin and gold paper. Glue a brooch pin to the back of the brooch. Craft shops sell jewellery components.

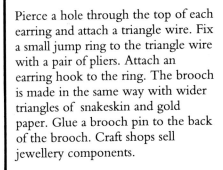

REGENCY SILHOUETTE

POT OF ANEMONES

Give your home a period touch with this classic decoration. You can use a clear profile sketch or a photograph as a basis for your picture. Make a tracing of the outline and place it face down on the back of a piece of black paper. Redraw the design to transfer it.

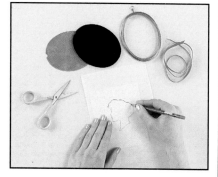

Cut out the motif with a pair of small, sharp scissors and glue the design to white paper. Trim the paper to fit your frame. Place the picture in the frame and glue a small ribbon bow to the top.

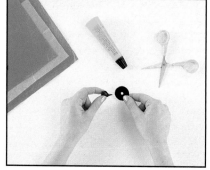

This delightful picture will brighten a dreary day. Cut a 3cm (1¼in) diameter circle of black paper; cut a fringe around the edge and a small hole in the centre. Cut a 6cm (2¼in) diameter circle of black tissue paper and wrap it over a small ball of cotton wool (absorbent cotton). Twist the edges together and insert into the hole.

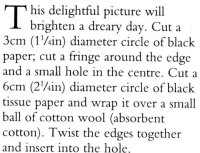

Use the template on page 25 to cut six petals from tissue paper and glue to the twisted end. Make two more flowers. Glue some striped wallpaper to a piece of cardboard and some cream paper over the lower third. From thick brown paper, cut a rectangle 13cm x 10cm (5in x 4in) for the pot and a strip 15cm x 2.5cm (6in x 1in) for the rim.

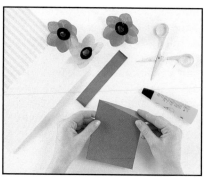

On one long edge of the pot mark 2.5cm (1in) from each end. Draw a line from the marks to the top corners and fold back the ends along the lines. Fold under 5mm (¼in) at the ends of the rim. Glue the folded ends of the pot to the background, slightly bowing the pot outwards. Glue the rim over the top in the same way. Glue flowers in place above the pot.

T he right mount can really enhance a picture. Buy a plain cardboard mount to fit your picture. Draw a 1cm (³⁄₈in) wide border around the window with a pencil. Cut four 1cm (³⁄₈in) wide strips of marbled paper. Spray the back of one strip with spray glue and place on the border. Cut off the ends diagonally at the corners with a craft knife.

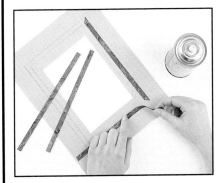

Apply the other strips to the mount, cutting the ends to meet diagonally in a mitred corner.

T o make these smart frames, cut two pieces of mounting board 25cm x 19cm (10in x 7½in). Cut a window 17cm x 11cm (7in x 4½in) in the centre of one piece. Cut two pieces of giftwrap to cover the frames. Lay the window mount on the wrong side of one piece and cut a window in the giftwrap, leaving a 2cm (³⁄₄in) margin. Snip to the corners and glue the margins down.

To complete the mount, draw a line each side of the border with a fine-tipped gold pen.

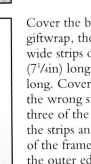

Cover the back of the frame with giftwrap, then cut two 1cm (³⁄₈in) wide strips of mounting board 18cm (7¼in) long and one 22cm (8½in) long. Cover with paper and glue to the wrong side of the back just inside three of the edges. Spread glue on the strips and carefully place the front of the frame on top, checking that the outer edges are level.

Cut a rectangle of mounting board 18cm x 6cm (7¼in x 2¼in) for the stand. Score across the stand 5cm (2in) from one end. Cover the stand with giftwrap and glue the scored end to the back with the other end level with either a long or short side depending on whether your photo is in landscape or portrait form. Bend the stand outwards.

Drop two or three colours onto the water and swirl together with the end of a paint brush. Cut plain paper to fit the tray. Wearing rubber gloves, start at one end of the tray and lower the paper onto the surface of the water so it can pick up the pattern. Carefully lift up the paper.

Leave the paper to dry overnight on newspaper. You can remove the paint from the tray by drawing strips of newspaper across the surface of the water.

The marbled paper can be used in many ways. Here, a plain book takes on a sophisticated look when recovered. Cut a rectangle of marbled paper large enough to wrap around the book with a 2.5cm (1in) margin on all sides. Wrap the paper around the book, open the cover and glue the paper inside the opening edges.

Prop up the book so the cover is open at a right angle. Snip the paper each side of the spine and stick the top and bottom margin inside the covers, folding under the corners.

T here are many methods for marbling paper but this way needs little equipment. Fill a shallow tray with water. Put spots of enamel paint on the water with a paint brush. If they sink the paint is too thick and needs thinning with a little white spirit. If they disperse into a faint film it is too thin and should be mixed with more paint.

Push the paper at the ends of the spine between the spine and the pages with the points of a pair of scissors. Arrange jewellery stones on the cover and use a strong glue to stick them in place. Cut two pieces of paper to fit inside the covers and glue inside.

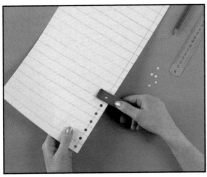

Co-ordinate your home with a pleated lampshade to match the wallpaper. For a 30cm (12in) wide shade cut a strip of wallpaper 130cm x 20cm (51in x 8in). On the wrong side, rule pleat lines across the strip 2cm (¾in) apart then draw a line along the length 1.2cm (½in) from the top. Punch a hole on this line between each pleat line.

Fold the strip in concertina pleats along the pleat lines. On the wrong side, slide each pleat into the punch in turn and make half a hole on the fold on the line. These holes will rest on the top section of the frame when the lampshade is finished.

Overlap the ends of the lampshade and thread ribbon through the holes in the middle of each pleat. Draw up the pleats and slip the lampshade over the frame, resting the notches on top of the frame. Pull the ribbon ends to tighten the top and tie in a decorative bow.

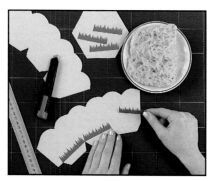

Fill this pretty basket with tiny sweet eggs to delight a child at Easter. Using the templates on page 25 cut out two sides and a base in pale blue cardboard and the grass in green gummed paper. Lightly score the sides of the basket along the broken lines with a craft knife, then stick on the grass.

Fold the sides backwards along the scored lines and join end to end in a ring by gluing each end tab under the opposite end of the other side. Glue the base under the base tabs. Cut a strip of pale blue cardboard for the handle measuring 30cm x 1cm (12in x ³/₈in). Stick the ends inside the basket.

Cut out two rabbits (see page 25) in brown cardboard. Glue a ball of cotton wool (absorbent cotton) to the rabbits as bobtails. Cut two strips of pale blue cardboard 4cm x 1cm (1¹/₂in x ³/₈in) and fold them widthwise in half to make hinges. Glue one half to the back of the rabbit matching the fold to the broken line. Glue the other half to the basket under the handles.

There is no excuse for mislaying letters with this smart letter rack. From thick mounting board cut a rectangle 24cm x 8cm (9½in x 3¼in) for the front and 24cm x 10cm (9½in x 4in) for the back. Diagonally trim away the top corners and cover one side of each piece with giftwrap.

Cut giftwrap slightly smaller than the front and back sections and glue in position on the wrong side. Take a piece of wood 24cm (9½in) long by 3cm (1¼in) wide and 1cm (³⁄₈in) thick. Cover the wood with coloured paper.

Cut a rectangle of mounting board 27cm x 7cm (10½in x 2¾in) for the base and cover with coloured paper. Use a strong glue to stick the front to one narrow edge of the wood keeping the lower edges level. Glue the back to the other side in the same way. Finish the letter rack by gluing this upper section centrally to the base.

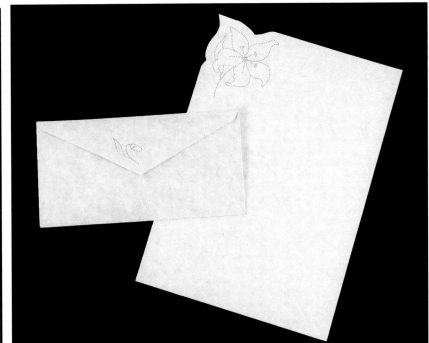

Stylish and original stationery is expensive to buy but this delicate design is cheap and easy to produce. Draw a simple motif on layout paper then retrace the design on the other side. Place your drawing on the top left-hand corner of a sheet of writing paper about 1cm (³⁄₈in) inside the edges. Redraw the motif to transfer it to the writing paper.

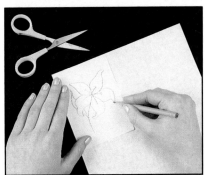

Now prick along the lines with a needle or pin. You may find it helpful to practise on a scrap of paper first to judge how far apart the pinpricks should be.

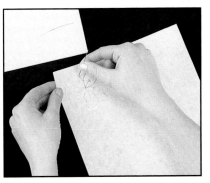

Rub out the pencil lines then trim away the corner of the paper to echo the shape of the design. Pinprick a co-ordinating motif on the matching envelope flap.

Revive the Victorian hobby of découpage and decorate a box with pretty paper pictures. Cut out suitable pictures from greeting cards or magazines or use reproductions of Victorian prints.

Make this carrier bag and you have a gift bag for your presents or go a step further and make the bag itself the present. Cut a piece of thick yellow cardboard 57.5cm x 29cm (22⅝in x 11½in). Refer to the diagram on page 25 and score along the solid and broken lines. Cut away the lower right-hand corner and cut into the base along the solid lines.

Arrange the pictures on the box and then stick them in place with spray glue. Smooth in place.

Fold the bag forwards along the solid lines and backwards along the broken lines. Turn the bag over and, with a pencil, lightly divide the front into quarters. Cut out a small hole at the centre for the clockwork. Cut out four pieces of red paper 1.5cm x 1cm (⅝in x ⅜in) and glue on the divisions 7cm (2¾in) from the hole.

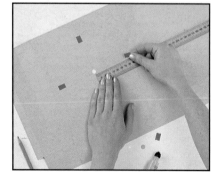

Apply a thin coat of clear gloss varnish all over the box and lid. Leave to dry and then sand lightly with fine sandpaper. Build up about six layers of varnish, sanding the box between each coat.

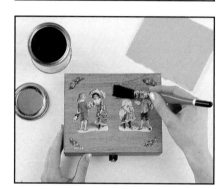

Rub out the pencil lines. Join the side seam by gluing the narrow tab under the opposite end. Fold under the small base sections then glue the long sections underneath. Cut two strips of green cardboard for handles 30cm x 1cm (12in x ⅜in). Glue the ends inside the top of the bag. Insert the clockwork rod through the hole and attach the hands.

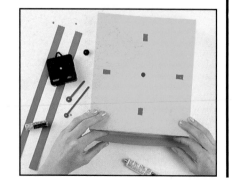

You could even decorate a simple DIY pine letter rack to match, for a lovely gift or a smart desk accessory. Sand the wood smooth and cut out two stencil sheets from the small curved rope design opposite. Tape the first stencil on to the wood and use quick-drying stencil paints, mixed up to match your decor, to stencil the first half of your design.

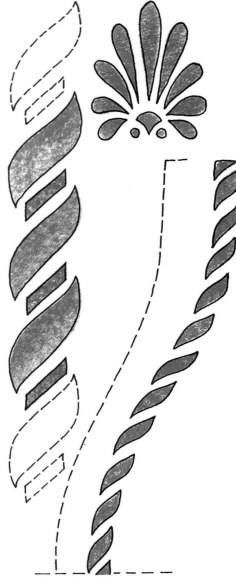

H and painted notepaper and envelopes make a stylish and original gift. Use the stencils shown here to decorate the top of some sheets, working with oil-based stencil crayons. Rub a little crayon on to a corner of the stencil or a spare piece of acetate and then collect the colour on to a brush. Stencil the colour on to the paper using a circular movement.

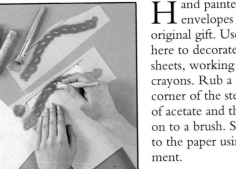

Match up the remainder of the design on the second stencil sheet and paint the second colour. Temporarily assemble the four walls of the letter rack with tape and stencil the large rope design (see above right) around the lower edge of the box in the same colours.

Above: Use these patterns to cut out your stencils for the letter rack and notepaper. The curved rope pattern only shows half of the design, so trace it off marking on the straight dotted centre line. Then turn the tracing over, match up the design, and trace in the other half accurately.

Decorate envelopes to match using the stencil crayons. Use a simple design along the lower edge or just a single motif that will not get in the way of the written address. Leave the stencilling to set for a while before using the notepaper and envelopes, to avoid smudging.

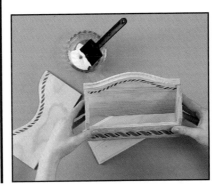

Now glue the box together using PVA wood glue. Begin with the four walls, then, when dry, glue these to the base. The centre section will then just slide into place. Glue this if you wish. Varnish the letter rack with several coats of clear polyurethane varnish to give a smooth, durable finish and to protect the stencilling.

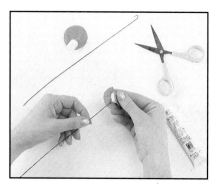

Take a length of thick wire and bend the end into a hook. Glue a small ball of cotton wool (absorbent cotton) over the hook. Cut a 4cm (1⅝in) diameter circle of green crepe paper. Wrap the circle over the ball and glue the edges around the wire. Cut two 3.5cm (1½in) diameter circles of black crepe paper and cut a fringe around the edge of each circle.

Make a hole through the centre of the black circles and insert the wire through the holes, push the circles up to the green ball. Use the template on page 25 to cut out six petals in red crepe paper with the arrow along the grain of paper. Pull the top of the petals between thumb and finger to flute the edges.

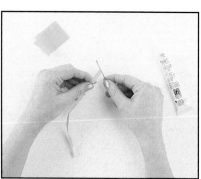

Glue the base of three petals under the poppy centre then glue the remaining petals in between. Bind the wire with a thin strip of green crepe paper and glue the ends in place to complete.

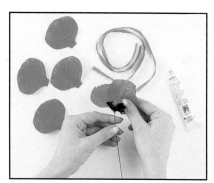

To make a daffodil, bend a 12cm (4¾in) length of thin wire in half for the stamen. Starting at the bent end, bind the wire with a narrow strip of yellow crepe paper. Secure the ends with a dab of glue. Cut yellow crepe paper 6cm x 4cm (2¼in x 1⅝in) with the grain running along the short edges. Pull one long edge between thumb and finger to flute the edge.

Overlap the ends of the rectangle and glue together making the trumpet. Place the stamen in the trumpet and gather the lower edge tightly with thread. Using the template on page 25 cut six petals in yellow crepe paper with the grain running parallel with the arrow. Stretch the petals across their width.

Dab glue on the base of the petals and stick to the base of the trumpet. Place the stamen end against a length of thick wire and bind together with a narrow strip of green crepe paper; glue the ends in place then bend the flowerhead forward. Fold strips of thick green paper in half lengthwise for leaves and cut pointed ends.

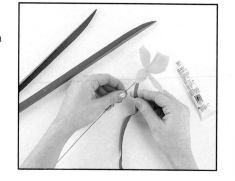

A zany idea for an unusual ornament or table centrepiece. For the apples fold a 12cm (4³/₄in) square of thin cardboard in half and draw half an apple shape against the fold. Cut out the apple then open out the cardboard to use as a template. Cut a total of 48 apples in light green and red tissue paper. Mix the colours and sew the pieces together along the centre.

Lift up the apple halves on one side except the bottom one. Dab glue on the bottom half close to the edge in the centre and then each side between the centre and stitching. Press down the next half and dab glue close to the edge between the first positions. Continue to the top tissue layer, alternating positions.

Glue the other half of the apple in the same way. Cut a stalk and leaf in green cardboard and glue to the top of the apple. Dab glue close to the edge in the centre and then either side between the centre and the stitching. Carefully press the two halves together and then glue the back halves together in the same way.

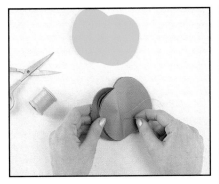

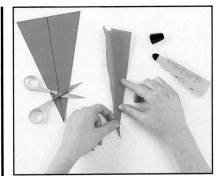

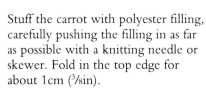

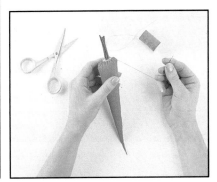

To make the carrots, draw a T shape on paper, the horizontal line 13cm (5in) long and the vertical line 20cm (8in) long. Join the lines together in a triangle. Cut out the triangle in orange crepe paper. Spread glue sparingly along one edge. Gently press the other long edge onto the glue and leave to dry.

Stuff the carrot with polyester filling, carefully pushing the filling in as far as possible with a knitting needle or skewer. Fold in the top edge for about 1cm (³/₈in).

Cut two strips of green crepe paper 10cm x 3cm (4in x 1¹/₄in), cutting the length along the grain. Roll the strips tightly lengthwise and glue along the long edges. Cut the strips in half. Hold the ends of these stalks inside the carrot and gather the folded edge tightly around the ends. Fasten the threads securely.

S tencil this attractive iris design on to thick watercolour paper for a linen texture and use wax stencil crayons for subtle colour shading. Size up the design and cut three stencils for mauve, yellow and green areas. Tape the green stencil in place and blend together two green crayons. Rub the crayons on to the acetate and then collect the colour on to the brush.

Remove the green stencil and tape the mauve one in position, lining up the vertical and horizontal marks. Blend mauve, blue and turquoise for the flowers, shading the lower petals in mauve and the upper ones in blues, and getting deeper towards the centre of each flower. Lastly, use the yellow stencil. Work the brush in a light circular motion to shade the colours throughout.

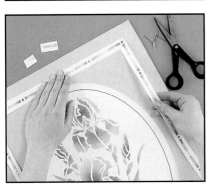

Have an oval mount cut to fit around your stencil. Cut out the border stencil from the design shown opposite and try it out on scrap paper in various colours. Cut these trial pieces into strips and lay them around your mount. Hold them in place with masking tape and then insert a pin centrally at each corner when you are happy with the position.

Carefully remove the strips and, very lightly, mark guide lines for stencilling the border using a pencil and set-square. Check the lines are exactly the right distance from the oval shape and parallel to the outer edge. The stencils at the top and sides should be equidistant from the oval and the lower stencil slightly further away to look visually correct.

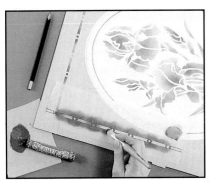

Finally, stencil the border in a single colour using stencil crayons as before. Build up the colour where the strips meet the round spots in the design to add interest. Assemble the stencil with the mount and a piece of glass in a simple frame coloured to complement your flowers and decorations.

Suggested size: One square represents 2.5cm (1in).

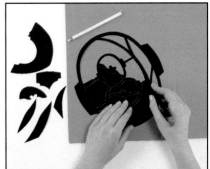

Hang this Oriental mobile at a window and watch the sun shine through the coloured tissue paper. Use the template on page 25 to cut out a pair of lanterns in black cardboard. Cut out all the sections, taking care not to cut through any of the 'bridges'.

To achieve the stained glass effect, cut out coloured tissue paper a little larger than the sections to be covered. Glue the pieces of tissue paper to the back of one lantern. Trim the edges. Glue a silky red tassel to hang from the bottom of one lantern at the centre. Now glue the two lanterns together enclosing the tissue paper. Suspend the mobile on red embroidery thread.

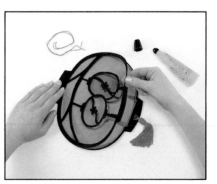

Here are templates and diagrams for several of the projects in the preceeding chapter. These need to be enlarged as follows: draw a grid of 3cm (1¼in) squares, then copy the design onto your grid, square by square, using the lines as a guide.

The clock is constructed from measurements. Use a ruler and set square to draw the shape onto cardboard and follow either the metric or imperial measurements but not a combination of the two.

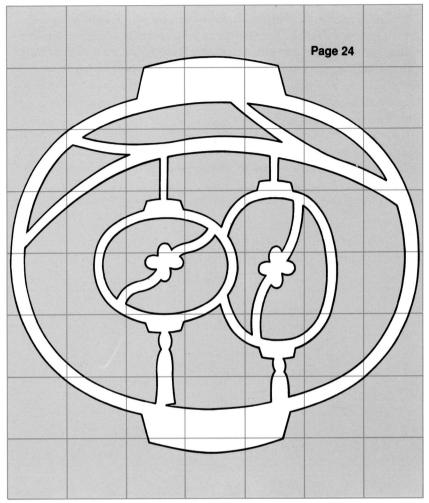

Page 24

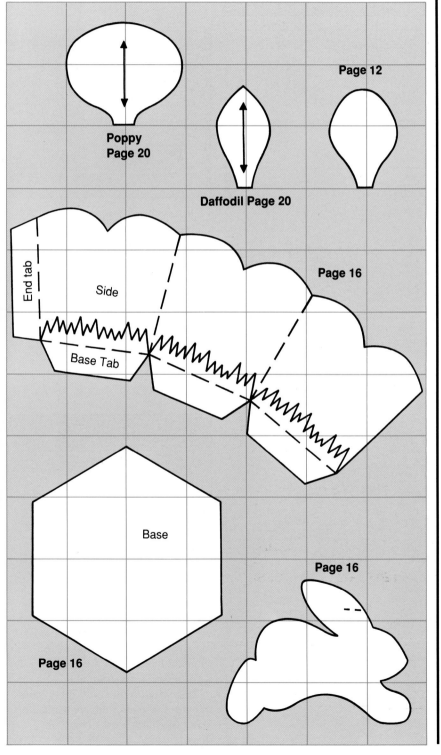

Page 12

**Poppy
Page 20**

Daffodil Page 20

End tab

Side

Base Tab

Page 16

Base

Page 16

Page 16

Page 16

Page 18

20cm (8¼in) 3.5cm (1⅜in) 3.5cm (1⅜in) 20cm (8¼in) 3.5cm (1⅜in) 3.5cm (1⅜in)

Back

Front

4cm (1⅝in)

5cm (2in)

Base

DESIGNS FOR CHILDREN

T his chapter is bursting with colourful and fun designs which children can make themselves: a jolly elephant mobile, cheeky refrigerator magnets and artistic lakeside collage are all straightforward yet challenging for young minds. There is also a host of toys and ornaments to brighten up children's rooms which most adults will enjoy making themselves. All the necessary patterns have been provided on pages 38-39.

Do ensure that children are supervised if cutting out is involved. Most paper items can be successfully cut using children's safety scissors, but tougher cardboard may need to be cut by an adult with a craft knife.

H ere is a mobile for animal lovers – a small herd of elephants. Cut out four elephants in co-ordinating coloured cardboard using the template on page 38. Draw eyes on both sides with a felt-tipped pen and cut slits along the broken lines with a craft knife. Make a hole with a thick needle at the top of the elephant.

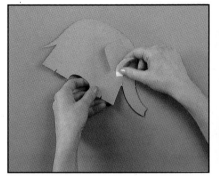

Make a pattern of the ear and tusk. Fold coloured cardboard in half and place the ear pattern on top, matching the broken line to the fold. Draw around the ear and cut it out. Cut out the tusks in white cardboard in the same way. Insert the ears and tusks halfway through the slits and bend them downwards.

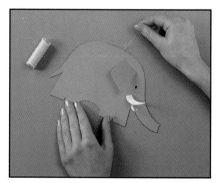

Cut four 45cm (18in) lengths of thread. Loop the threads in half and insert the ends through the hole. Pull the ends through the loop so the elephant hangs from the thread. Knot the ends together and hang on mobile wires. You could spray paint the wires to match the elephants. Hang the mobile on a length of thread.

Now you can have your very own prehistoric monster – a Stegosaurus dinosaur. Refer to the template on page 38 to make a pattern of the dinosaur body and two sets of legs on thin cardboard. Draw around the patterns onto mounting board (use a board that is six sheets thick). Cut out the sections with a craft knife.

Slot the legs and body together, placing the smaller set of legs at the front, as shown.

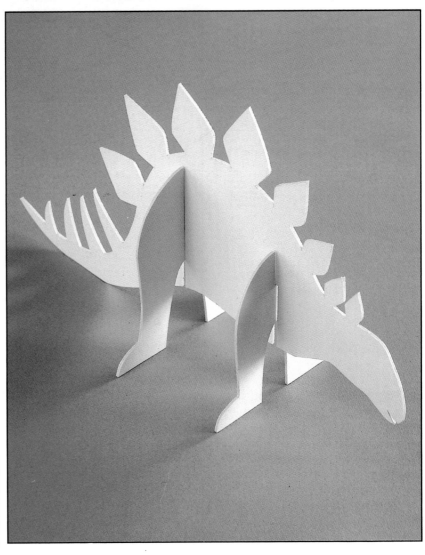

What better way to invite friends to a party at the local hop than with this funny frog. Draw a frog with large, bulging eyes on thin green cardboard and cut it out. Cut out a narrow smiling mouth.

Glue on a pair of joggle eyes and write a message on the back. Now all you need is the party . . .

These funny glasses are sure to amuse all who see them. Cut a pattern using the template on page 39 and use to cut a blue cardboard front. Cut out the windows and use as a guide to cut two lenses from green transparent acetate, adding 1cm (³⁄₈in) to the edges all round. Glue the lenses behind the windows.

Textured papers make an interesting collage. Cut pale blue cardboard 30cm x 24cm (12in x 9¹⁄₂in) for the background. Cover the lower 11cm (4¹⁄₄in) with clear sticky-backed plastic. Cut a strip of pale green cardboard and tear away one long edge. Glue the strip above the 'lake'. Cut pointed strips of green gummed paper and stick over the join.

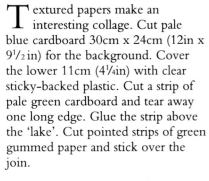

Use the template to cut out a pair of palm trees – cut the trunks in brown cardboard and leaves in green cardboard. Glue the palm trees each side of the front piece.

Use the template on page 39 to cut out the swan and wing in wavy textured paper. Cut the beak in orange paper and glue behind the swan. Draw the swan's eye with a black felt-tipped pen. Glue the swan to the middle of the lake and glue the wing on top.

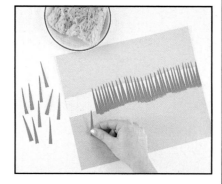

Cut out a pair of arms in blue cardboard using the template. Score the ends along the broken lines and bend back the tabs at right angles. Glue the tabs behind the glasses to complete.

Cut very thin strips of brown cardboard for the bullrush stems and three long leaves from green crepe paper. Glue the leaves and stems to the picture. Cut bullrushes from black flock sticky-backed plastic and glue over the top of the stems. Use the template to cut out three lily pads in green cardboard and glue to the lake.

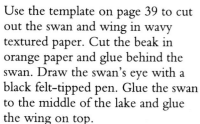

A COOL CHARACTER

C ast a spooky glow at a Halloween gathering with this eerie lantern. Cut a strip 50cm x 22cm (20in x 8½in) of shiny black cardboard – the sort that is white on the other side. Cut out a large and a small bat from thin cardboard and use as templates to draw three bats on the back of the strip.

When you have finished tracing the bats, carefully cut them out using a craft knife.

T his jolly hippo will brighten the kitchen when stuck to the fridge door with a small magnet. Roughly cut out a design from some left-over wrapping paper. Stick the motif to a piece of thick cardboard with spray glue.

Overlap the ends of the strip and staple them together. To complete the effect, place a few nightlights inside the lantern. Do not leave the lantern unattended when it is lit.

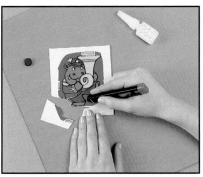

Cut out the picture with a craft knife. Do not attempt to cut right through the board in one go, but gradually cut deeper and deeper until you reach the cutting board.

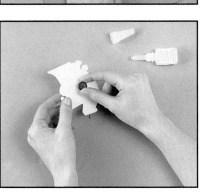

Glue a fridge magnet to the back of the character. Magnets are available at many art and craft shops.

This is a traditional kite with a difference – there is an amusing clown's face on the front. To make the frame you will need two lengths of wood dowel; one 84cm (33in) long and the other 56cm (22in). Cut two small notches 5mm (¼in) from the ends of both sticks with a craft knife.

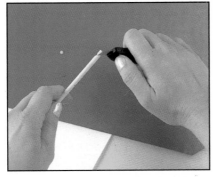

Mark the short stick at the centre and the long stick 28cm (11in) from one end. Lay the sticks across one another at right angles matching the marks, and bind tightly with fine string. Secure with a dab of glue. Tie string around the notches at one end of a stick, then wind it tightly around the other notches as shown and knot the ends of string together.

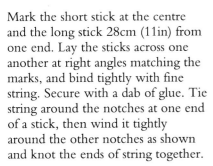

Butt the edges of a white and a green piece of paper together with the wrong sides uppermost. Lay the kite frame on top and cut around it 1.5cm (⅝in) outside the string. Cut off the corners level with the notches. Remove the frame and join the butted edges together with masking tape.

Apply double-sided tape to the edges of the kite covering on the wrong side. Place the frame on top and fold over the edges enclosing the string.

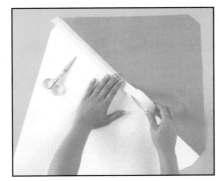

Cut a 112cm (44in) length of string and tie the ends to the top and bottom notch. Cut a 92cm (36¼in) length and tie the ends to the side notches. Balance the kite by resting the strings on a finger and fastening them together with a curtain ring where they cross over. Decorate the front with ribbons and paper shapes. Finally, tie a ball of string to the ring.

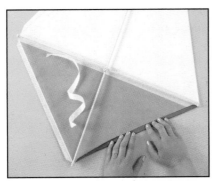

The method for making this traditional pinwheel is Origami, which is the ancient Japanese craft of paper folding. Start with a 20cm (8in) square of patterned paper. Fold the side edges to meet at the centre then fold the top and bottom edges to meet at the centre as well.

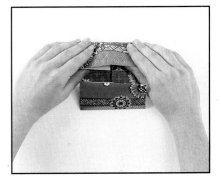

Now bring the side corners at the centre to the top and bottom edges with a diagonal fold.

Open the diagonal folds out flat then lightly hold at the centre and pull each corner of the square underneath to the outside. Turn alternate points in opposite directions to form the pinwheel. Attach the pinwheel to a painted balsa wood stick with a drawing pin.

You can peer around corners and over walls with this smart periscope. Follow the diagram on page 39 to draw the periscope onto thick cardboard. Cut out the shape with a craft knife and score along the solid lines.

Bend the periscope backwards along the scored lines so you can see how it will look when finished. Flatten out the periscope and glue a small make-up mirror on the wrong side in the middle of the base and top.

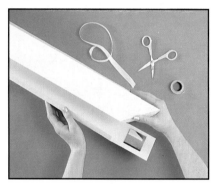

Bend the periscope back into shape and stick the long tab under the opposite long edge with double-sided tape.

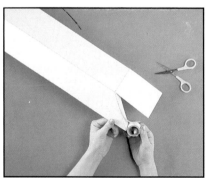

Stick the remaining tabs to the base and top with double-sided tape.

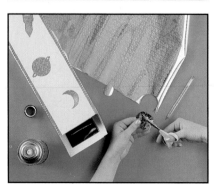

Apply decorative sticky tape over all the folds to neaten and reinforce the edges. Cut out space rockets and planets from giftwrap and stick to the periscope with spray glue.

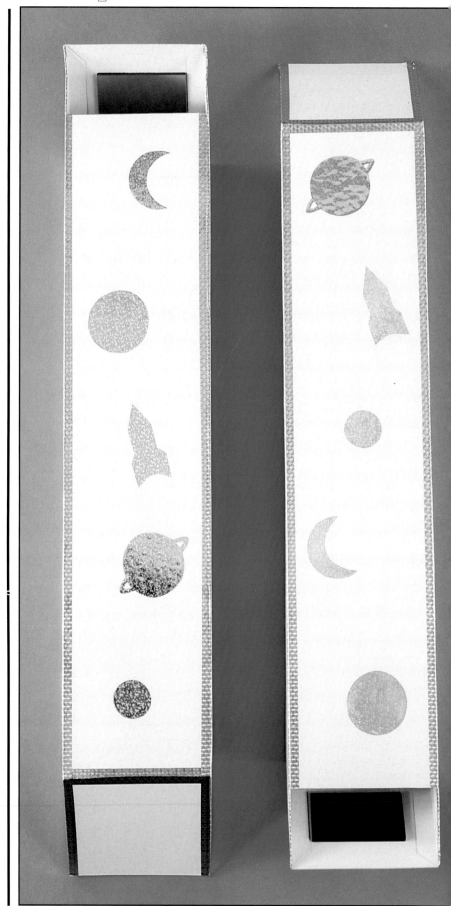

This clown is fun to make and not as difficult as he may seem. First cut a rectangle of crepe paper for the body 30cm x 24cm (12in x 9½in). Overlap the shorter edges and glue them together making a tube. Push toy filling inside and stuff the tube firmly. With a needle and thread, gather the open ends tightly, enclosing the filling.

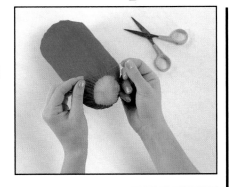

Cut two 14cm (5½in) squares of crepe paper for the sleeves and make two tubes like the body. For the arms, cut two pink pipecleaners 16cm (6¼in) long. Insert each arm into a sleeve and glue across one end, sandwiching the arm in the middle. Gently push toy filling inside around the arm.

Bend over the end of the arms in a hook to imitate hands. Gather the sleeves tightly above the hands with a needle and thread, making a frilled edge. Glue the flat ends of the sleeves to the body.

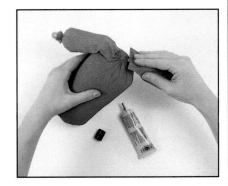

Cut a strip of crepe paper 35cm x 6cm (14in x 2¼in), cutting the short ends parallel with the grain of the crepe paper. This will be the neck ruffle. Glue the ends together and gather one long edge. Pull up the gathers tightly like a rosette and glue the ruffle on top of the body.

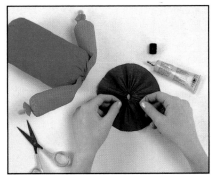

Take a 7cm (2¾in) diameter cotton pulp ball and glue a red bead in the middle for a nose. Draw eyes and a mouth with felt-tipped pens. Glue curly gift wrapping ribbon each side of the face. The hat is a 14cm (5½in) diameter circle of coloured cardboard. Cut to the centre and overlap the edges making a cone. Glue the edges together and glue the hat in place.

Glue the head on top of the ruffle. Using the template on page 39, cut out the shoes in coloured cardboard. Glue the body on top of the shoes and then glue some bright pom-poms to the hat, shoes and front of the body. This clown is not for playing with but is a charming ornament for a child's room.

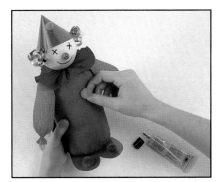

T his lion mask is made from papier-mâché moulded over a balloon. Blow up the balloon and tie a knot in the end. Tear newspaper into small pieces and then dilute PVA medium with water to thin it slightly. Spread a little of the solution on the front of the balloon and cover with the newspaper pieces.

Cover one half of the balloon with about seven layers of papier-mâché and leave to dry overnight. Gently pull the balloon away from the mask and trim the edges of the mask with a pair of scissors. Cut out two round holes for the eyes. Paint the mask with non-toxic ochre coloured paint and then paint a black nose and muzzle, as shown.

To make the mane, cut brown crepe paper 140cm x 16cm (55in x 6¼in) and fold lengthwise in half. Cut a fringe along the long edges. With a needle and long length of thread, gather up the mane close to the fold. Glue the mane around the lion's face. Finally, staple a length of thin elastic to each side of the back of the mask, to fit.

Make this colourful head-dress and join the tribe! Cut a 4cm (1½in) wide strip of red cardboard 60cm (24in) long. Cut out simple shapes from coloured papers and glue to the strip.

Overlap the ends of the strip and glue together. Stick three coloured quill feathers upright behind the strip with sticky tape.

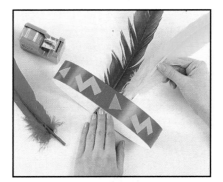

Although a bit more complicated to make than a cardboard mask, this mask will last much longer. The face is made from papier-mâché (see page 34 for instructions); the mould is a balloon. Blow the balloon up as big as you can without bursting it, and build up the papier-mâché over at least one half. When it is dry, gently let the air out of the balloon by piercing the knotted end.

Cut six 2.5cm (1in) wide strips of black crepe paper 40cm (16in) long. Spread paper glue along one long edge and fold the strips in half. Staple three lengths together at one end and make a plait. Bind the end with embroidery thread and make another plait in the same way. Stick the plaits to each side of the head-dress with sticky tape.

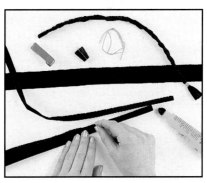

Trim the mask down, cutting the pointed end into a forehead. Cut out circular eyes and a curved mouth. Now give the mould a coat of white emulsion (water-based paint), sand it down and give it another two coats to make it as smooth a surface as possible.

Around each eye paint four slightly triangular stripes. Also paint large red lips and cheeks on either side. For the nose, paint a ping pong ball red and glue it in place. For the hair, cut short lengths of yarn and attach them to strips of sticky tape; stick these to the back of the mask. Finally, take a piece of elastic, staple it to either side, and paint over the staples with a touch more emulsion.

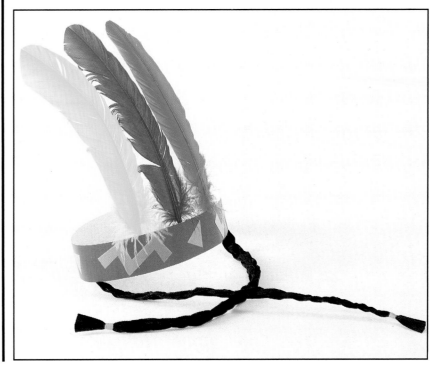

Create this unusual birthday table decoration, using the template on page 39 to cut a base and lid in white cardboard. Cut the end tab off the lid. Now cut a strip of mottled brown cardboard 30cm x 6cm (12in x 2¼in). Tear a thin strip of shiny red paper and glue along the middle of the 'sponge'. Score across the strip at the centre and 1.5cm (⅝in) from the ends.

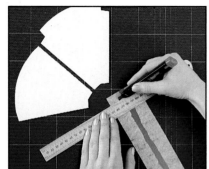

Score the base and lid along the broken lines and snip the end tab to the scored line. Bend all the pieces backwards along the scored lines. Glue the 'sponge' to the side tabs on the base with the folds at the corners. Cut pale blue cardboard 12cm x 6cm (4¾in x 2¼in) and glue one long edge over the end tabs.

Cut two 12cm (4¾in) long strips of white cardboard and cut scallops along one edge. Glue to the blue end as icing. Glue one tab of the lid inside the top of the box. Cut a strip of blue cardboard for the candle. Make a 'flame' from a foil sweet (candy) wrapper and glue to one end. Fold under the other end of the candle and glue to the lid.

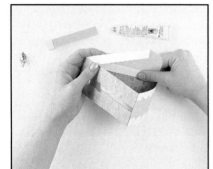

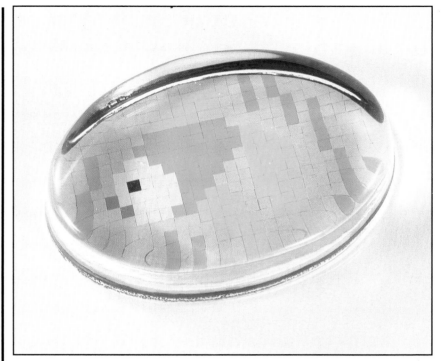

Glass paperweights such as these (available in kit form from craft shops) are ideal for making novel presents. Kids in particular will enjoy making this design. To work out a mosaic picture, draw a grid of squares about 4mm (³⁄₁₆in) apart. Trace around the paperweight template onto the grid and draw a design. Colour the picture as a guide for the finished mosaic.

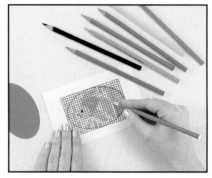

Cut out tiny squares of coloured paper the same size as the grid squares. Draw a cross on a piece of paper to help keep the mosaic squares straight. Spread paper glue thinly along part of one line and press the squares in place. Nudge them into position with scissors or tweezers. Follow the grid design and glue on all the squares.

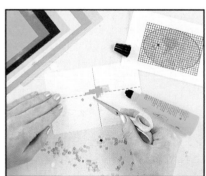

Use the paperweight template to cut the mosaic to fit the paperweight. Turn the paperweight upside down and lay the mosaic in the hollow. Peel the paper off the sticky-backed flock backing and carefully stick it over the back of the paperweight enclosing the mosaic.

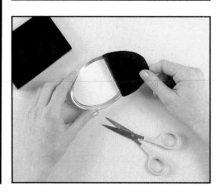

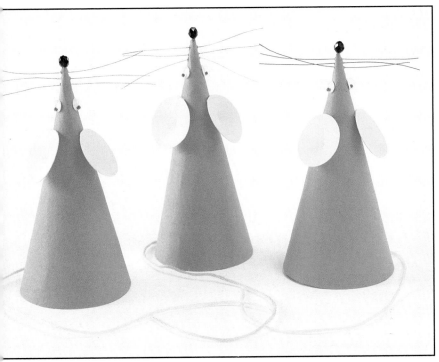

These amusing finger puppets are sure to entertain your friends. Use the template on page 39 to cut out the dancer in pale pink cardboard. Cut out the dress in shiny, deep pink cardboard and glue to the puppet. Next cut an 8cm (3in) diameter circle from the centre of a white paper doily for a petticoat and glue to the dress with spray glue.

Colour the hair, draw the eyes and lightly mark the nose with a black felt-tipped pen. Draw the mouth with a red felt-tipped pen and rouge the cheeks with a red coloured pencil.

Play to the gallery with this finger puppet trio of tiny friends. Cut out a quarter-circle of thin magenta cardboard with a 9cm (3½in) radius. Pull between thumb and finger to curve the piece. Overlap the straight edges to form a cone and glue the edges together.

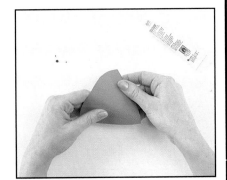

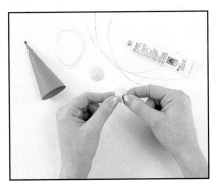

Mark the finger hole positions on the petticoat and carefully cut through all the layers with a craft knife.

Glue a small black bead to the point of the cone as a nose and then glue two small joggle eyes each side. To make the ears, cut out two small circles of thin pink cardboard. Cut to the centre and overlap the cut edges. Glue the overlapped edges together then glue the ears to the cone.

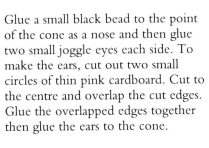

Take some toy-making whiskers and thread on a needle through the top of the cone. Drop a little glue onto the whiskers inside the cone to secure them. Trim the ends level. Thread a length of embroidery thread on a needle and attach to the base of the mouse at the back as a tail. Knot the thread inside the finger puppet.

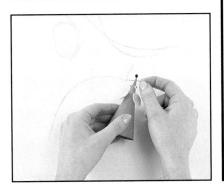

Size up patterns as described on page 25, making each square of your grid measure 3cm (1¼in).

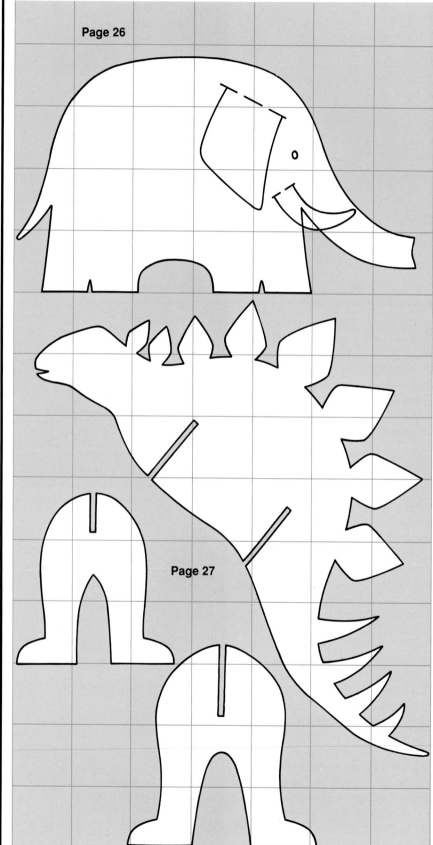

Page 26

Page 27

P apier-mâché is very durable and can be made in many ways. This traditional method uses a paste of flour and water. Tear up wallpaper lining paper into small pieces. Then grease the inside of a small bowl with Vaseline. Brush the paper pieces with paste and stick them inside the bowl, starting at the centre and working outwards.

Build up three layers of papier-mâché and leave to dry overnight. Apply at least four more layers. When the papier-mâché is completely dry, remove it from the bowl mould. Trim the top edge level with a pair of scissors. Paint the bowl with a craft paint, sanding between coats. Cut coloured tissue paper into small triangles.

Stick the triangles to the bowl with a clear varnish such as PVA medium. Once the bowl is decorated, coat it inside and out with the varnish. Line the bowl with tissue paper and fill it with pretty bathroom accessories.

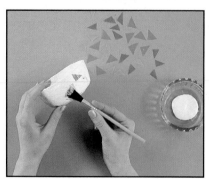

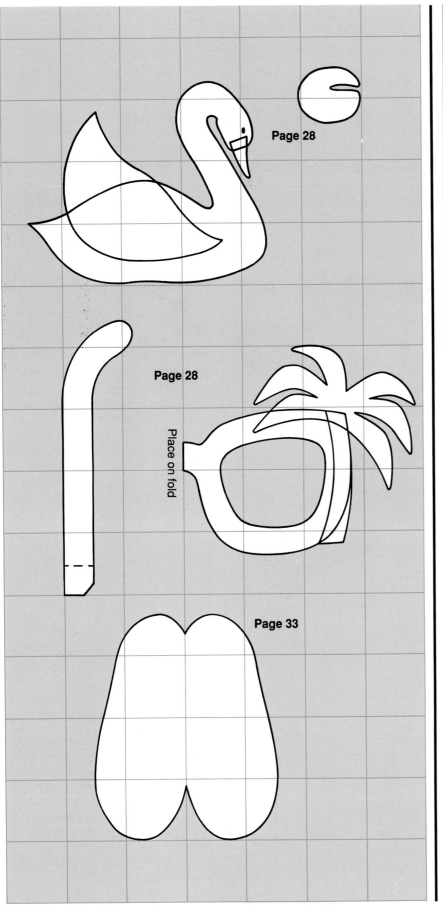

Page 28

Page 28

Place on fold

Page 33

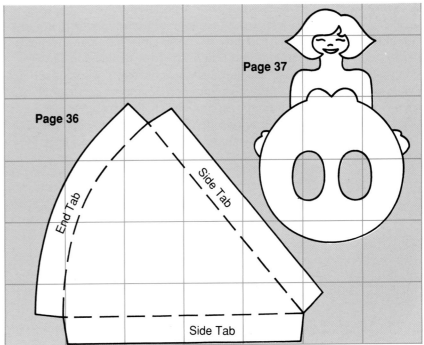

Page 36

End Tab

Side Tab

Side Tab

Page 37

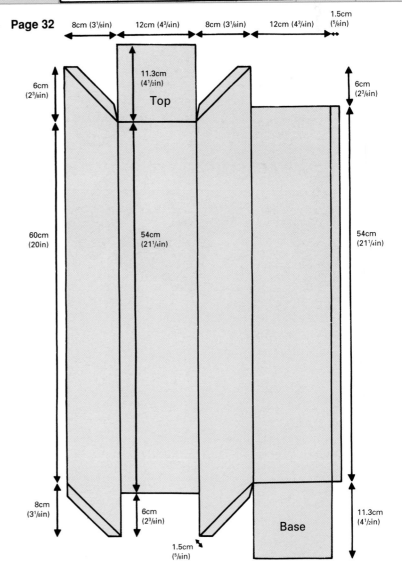

Page 32

8cm (3¹/8in) | 12cm (4³/4in) | 8cm (3¹/8in) | 12cm (4³/4in) | 1.5cm (⁵/8in)

6cm (2³/8in)

11.3cm (4¹/2in)

Top

6cm (2³/8in)

60cm (20in)

54cm (21¹/4in)

54cm (21¹/4in)

8cm (3¹/8in)

6cm (2³/8in)

1.5cm (⁵/8in)

Base

11.3cm (4¹/2in)

Don't spend a fortune buying party decorations, as this chapter will show you how to create a wide range of stunning effects at a low cost. From graceful paper garlands, to stylish fancy hats and jewelled masks, Christmas ornaments and festive wreaths, we include all that you might need to make your home look as festive as possible, and get everyone in the party mood. There are also designs to create your very own Advent Calendar, a pretty garland on which to hang your Christmas cards and a super winter sleigh to fill with sweets for a table centrepiece. Where possible we have included templates on page 59 to assist you.

Pull the cord and watch Santa dance. Use the template on page 59 to cut out the cardboard pieces. Cut one body and a pair of arms and legs from red cardboard. Mark the crosses on the back. Cut a pink face and glue to the head. Cut a white hat brim and beard, bobble and two cuffs. Glue the hat brim and beard over the face and the bobble to the top of the hat.

Cut out two green mittens, a black belt and two boots. Butt the straight ends of the mittens and arms together and glue cuffs over the joins. Wrap gold sticky tape around the middle of the belt and glue to the body. Glue the boot tops under the legs. Cut out a pink nose and glue on the face. Draw the eyes and mouth with felt-tipped pens.

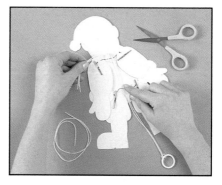

Mark dots on the limbs and attach to the body with paper fasteners at the crosses. Pull the limbs downwards on the back and tie the arms together with thread fastened through the dots. Tie the legs in the same way. Thread a small ring onto a double length of fine cord. Knot the cord around the legs' thread and then the arms' thread.

Cut a 3cm (1¼in) square of cardboard to use as a template for the doors. Draw around the square twenty-three times on the back of the tree, positioning the doors at random but leaving the trunk clear. Cut three sides of the doors, leave the right hand side 'hinged' so the door opens the right way on the other side.

On the right side of the tree, score the hinged side of each door lightly so it will open easily – but do not open the doors yet. Number the doors one to twenty-three with a silver pen.

Cut out small Christmas pictures from wrapping paper and used greeting cards. On the back of the tree, stick each picture behind a door by spreading paper glue on the tree around the doors.

Decorate the calendar with a gold star on the top and circles of metallic cardboard between the doors.

Write the number twenty-four on the front of a small red gift box with a silver pen. Stick a ribbon rosette on the top and glue the box onto the tree trunk. Fill the box with sweets. To finish, stick a picture hanger on the back of the calendar at the top.

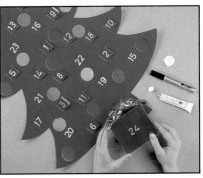

This Advent calendar can be used every year at Christmas. First make the Christmas tree pattern. Cut a piece of paper measuring about 63cm x 50cm (25in x 20in) and fold in half lengthwise. Draw half the tree with a trunk against the foldline and cut it out. Open out flat and use the pattern as a template to cut out the tree in green cardboard.

These miniature lanterns make attractive Christmas tree ornaments. First take a piece of foil-covered paper 11cm (5½in) square. Fold it in half, and rule a line 1.5cm (¾in) from the loose edges. Now rule lines 1cm (½in) apart, from the fold up to this first line. Cut along these lines and open out the sheet of paper.

If you haven't any shiny bells for the Christmas tree, it's not difficult to make some from foil, beads and a little string. First take a saucer and mark around it onto the back of some coloured foil. Cut out the circle, then fold it in half, and cut along the fold line. Fold each half of the circle into a cone and glue it in place.

Hold the paper with the cuts running vertically, and glue the two sides together. When this is firm, set the lantern on the table and gently push the top down to make the sides poke outwards.

For the clapper, string a bead onto a length of thread — preferably waxed — and tie a knot over the bead. Lay the thread against the bell so that the clapper is at the right level, then tie a knot level with the hole in the top. This prevents the string from being pulled through the hole when threaded. Pull the string through the hole from the inside and thread on a smaller bead at the top; knot in place.

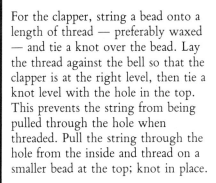

Finally, cut a strip of matching paper 13cm (5in) long and 1cm (½in) wide. Dab some glue on each end, and glue the strip onto the inside of the lantern, at the top, for a handle.

Finish each bell by dabbing a little glue around the bottom edge and sprinkling on some glitter. When you have made three bells, string them together, and attach them to a ring so that they can be hung on the tree. Wind a little tinsel wire around the string, and tie a couple of bows for that final touch of glamour.

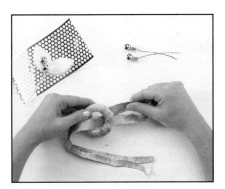

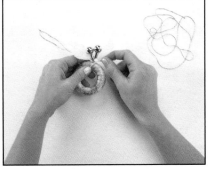

Add a touch of regal splendour to your tree with these golden decorations. To make a miniatrue wreath, first wind the wires of two silk leaves and two small glass balls together, and bind with white florists' tape. Cut a 16cm (6½in) length from sequin waste. Next cut a long strip of gold crepe paper, fold the edges in and bind around a small wooden ring.

Tie a loop of gold thread around the ring at the paper join. Twist the leaf and ball stems around the ring over the thread, folding in the wire ends to secure.

Fold the ends of the sequin waste into the centre so that they overlap, with the selvedges at each side. Thread a long length of fine florists' wire down the middle, through all the layers. Then thread the wire back and pull up gently to make a bow shape. Twist the wires tightly to secure and bind them around the leaf wires. Arrange the leaves, bow and balls attractively over the ring.

To make a jewelled sphere, first wrap a polystyrene ball with gold crepe paper: cut a square of paper to fit generously, and pull it up tightly over the ball. Tie firmly around the gathered paper with a length of gold thread, and knot the ends of the thread to make a hanging loop. Cut a strip of crepe paper to make a bow and fold the raw edges in. Pinch the strip into a bow shape.

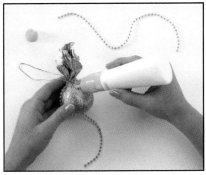

Run a line of clear adhesive around the ball and press a strip of beading trim into it. Repeat with a line of beading crossing in the opposite direction. Stick 'jewels' between the beads and large sequins, held in place with a pearl-headed pin. Trim the paper at the top of the sphere and attach the bow with a sequin trimmed pearl-headed pin.

From cartridge paper cut two rectangles, one 58cm x 10cm (23in x 4in), the other 58cm x 6.5cm (23in x 2½in). Mark each one into 12mm (½in) strips and draw a line 2.5cm (1in) from the long edge. Following your marks, cut out a zig-zag edge and pleat the strips. Use spray adhesive to stick gold foil to each side of the large rectangle, and silver foil to the smaller one.

Pleat the gold strip again and fold it into a circle. Join the two ends with double-sided tape or glue and prevent the centre from popping up by smearing glue into the centre. Weight down the star with a book until it is dry. Next make a loop from gold thread from which to hang the star, and glue this to the centre of the star at the back.

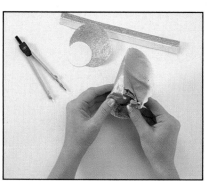

Make these delightful baskets to hang on your tree. Measure 4cm (1½in) up from the base of a yoghourt carton and cut round. Cut a 20cm (8in) diameter circle from crepe paper and cover the pot, stretching the paper up over the edges. Cover a cardboard circle with crepe paper to fit inside the base. Cut a handle 22cm (8½in) x 1.5cm (½in) from thin cardboard and cover.

Make up the silver star as before and place a double-sided adhesive pad on the centre back. Use this to attach the star to the gold star, aligning the pleats. Finally, put a little glue into the centre of the star and press a small glass ball in place.

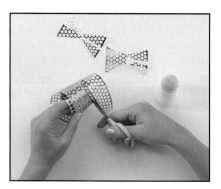

From sequin foil waste cut a strip long enough to wrap around the pot. Run a line of glue along the top and bottom of the pot and in one vertical line. Wrap the foil round, pressing into the glue, and trim, straightening the overlap along the vertical line of glue. Cut two strips 5cm (2in) wide from sequin waste, fold in half, selvedges level, and cut into bow shapes.

Staple the handle and foil bows each side of the basket. Tie bows from lengths of satin ribbon and stick over the foil bows with double-sided tape. Stick a double-sided adhesive pad in the bottom of the basket and arrange a bunch of glass balls on top.

Cut a 10cm (4in) diameter semi-circle of silver cardboard, silver crepe paper and crinkly film. Trim the curve of the film in zig-zags and flute the crepe paper curve between your thumb and finger. Place the crepe paper on the cardboard with the film on top and glue together along the straight edges. Overlap the straight edges in a cone and glue.

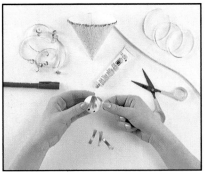

Draw eyes with a black pen on a 3.5cm (1½in) diameter cotton pulp ball. Cut short pieces of narrow giftwrap ribbon and glue to the head as a fringe. Cut longer pieces and pull the ends over a knife blade to curl them, then glue over the head. Glue ribbon around the head, then cut a slit in the base of the head and push the cone point through.

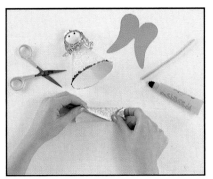

Cut silver crepe paper 11cm x 6cm (4½in x 2¼in) and flute the ends. Glue the long edges together and insert a 15cm (6in) pipecleaner for the arms through the tube and bend back the ends. Squeeze the centre and glue behind the cone, bending the arms forward. Use the template on page 59 to cut silver cardboard wings and glue them in place behind the angel.

To make these pretty silver bells cut out two bell shapes from cardboard. Peel the backing off some silver sticky-backed plastic and place the cut-outs on top, pressing firmly; then cut around them.

Glue the loops at the top of the bells together, spreading the bell shapes apart as shown.

Curl some gift wrap ribbon by running the blunt edge of a scissors blade along it; attach the ribbon to the bells. Finish off with a bow tied through the loops and some tiny birds cut from foil paper. The template for these is superimposed on the bell template.

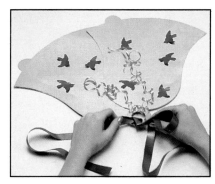

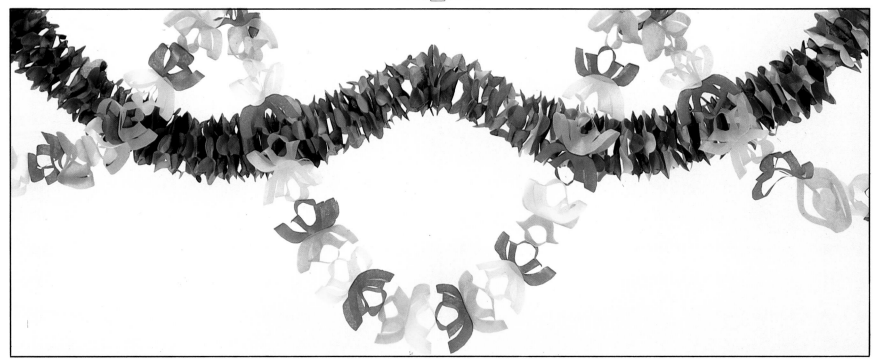

This graceful paper chain is made from circular pieces of tissue paper. First cut two circles of cardboard and lots of circles of tissue paper, all 10cm (4in) in diameter. Take about ten tissue paper circles and fold them together in four. If you use more than about ten layers, the folds won't be as good.

Now make two curved cuts as shown, from the single-folded edge almost to the double folds. Open out the circles. Glue the centre of the first circle to the middle of one cardboard circle.

Next, take the second tissue circle and glue it to the first at the top and bottom. Glue the third circle to the centre of the second circle. Continue in this way remembering to glue alternate circles in the same place at the top and bottom. If you alter the positioning you will spoil the effect. Finally glue the other cardboard circle to the last tissue circle to complete the garland.

Another simple garland made from tissue paper. Cut out a cardboard pattern from the template on page 59. Now cut out lots of flower shapes from tissue paper, using several different colours.

To start the garland, dab a little glue (one that won't soak through the thin paper) onto alternate petals of the first flower. Place the second flower on top and press them together.

Now on the second flower dab glue on the petals lying between those glued on the first flower. Take the third flower and press it firmly on top. Continue in this way, gluing petals in alternate positions, until the garland is long enough. Cut two extra cardboard shapes from the pattern and glue them to either end. Onto these tape a little loop of cord for hanging the garland.

This garland is made from different coloured tissue paper stars. Refer to the template on page 59 to make the basic pattern from thin paper. Fold up to six layers of tissue paper into quarters, place a quarter of the paper pattern on top, edges level, and cut out. Fold the tissue paper in half again, (separate some of the layers if too bulky) and cut two slits in the positions marked in the photograph below. Cut a collection of different coloured tissue paper 'stars' in this way, plus two stars cut from cartridge paper for the garland ends. Glue a tissue star to each paper star using spray adhesive. Stick a small piece of double-sided tape to the centre of one tissue star and press this onto the centre of the tissue-covered paper star.

Next, place double-sided tape on four opposite points of the tissue star, and stick another star on top, aligning the points and slits. Keep repeating the sequence, pressing pieces of double-sided tape alternately to the centre, then to the four points, of each star, building up the layers until the garland is the required length. Finish by attaching the other end section.

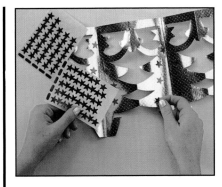

Use this attractive frieze to decorate shelves, or to hang along a wall. From a length of foil gift wrap cut a long strip 23cm (9in) wide. Make a tree template from paper using the pattern on page 59 and line it up along one short edge of the gift wrap. Draw around the outline marking a fold line down the centre of the tree shape. Mark an X on each section to be cut out.

Fold the gift wrap concertina fashion along its length and staple the layers together above and below the pattern area to prevent the folds from slipping. Cut out through all the layers, using a craft knife to cut out the enclosed areas between the star and the bell shapes. Be careful not to cut through the folds at the edge.

Open the frieze out. The foil can be left in gentle folds, or pressed flat with a cool iron. Stick self-adhesive foil stars all over the trees. You can make the frieze to the required length simply by joining several frieze strips together, end to end, with sticky tape.

To make this festive ring, cut a long strip of crepe paper from the length of the roll, and bind a 20cm (8in) embroidery ring, securing the ends with double-sided tape near the hanging loop. Cut narrow gold ribbon about 110cm (43in) long and wind around the ring, securing with tape. Cut the same length from a gold sequin strip and wind between the ribbon.

Cut a strip of red crepe paper 1m (40in) long and 20cm (8in) wide; fold in half lengthways. Cut the same length from sequin waste and place over the crepe strip. Bind the centre with a long piece of florists' wire and trim ends into V-shape. Measure 23cm (9in) each side of the centre, bind with wire and fold the strip into a bow shape, holding it in shape with an adhesive pad.

Use the trailing centre wires to secure the bow in position at the top of the ring and arrange the ribbon ends over the ring. Finally, wire three small glass balls together and wrap these around the bow centre.

H ang this everlasting wreath on the door for a warm welcome to your visitors. Cut 5cm (2in) squares of green crepe paper and stick a small piece of masking tape in the centre for extra strength. Cut the point off a cocktail stick and use to make holes in a polystyrene ring. Push each square into a hole with the blunt end of the stick.

Continue pushing in squares until the ring is hidden. Take some artificial red berries on wires and push them into the wreath at random to decorate.

Tie a large bow of red satin ribbon. Bend a length of wire into a 'U' shape and thread through the back of the bow. Push the ends of the wire into the wreath.

This is a fun and simple way to hang up your Christmas cards. Simply take three long pieces of gift wrap or woven ribbon in red, green and gold, and plait them tightly together. Knot them at each end to hold them in place.

Now take some clothes pegs, lay them on several sheets of newspaper and spray them with gold paint. Turn them until all the sides have been covered and leave them to dry.

Fasten the ribbon to the wall at each end, and use the gold pegs to attach your Christmas cards to it. (If you prefer, and if you have some to spare, you could use tinsel instead of ribbon.)

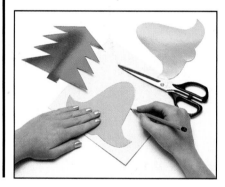

Here is a lovely sparkly garland to hang at Christmastime. If you want to make it for a birthday party instead, substitute little boxed gifts and bottles for the bells, and make trees in pastel colours. Cut the chosen shapes from foil-covered cardboard, marking them out on the wrong side. Be careful when cutting as foil cardboard tends to crinkle at the edges.

Make a tiny hole in the top of each, using a hole punch, or the tip of a skewer. Using red twine, tie each shape to a long strand of tinsel, leaving even spaces between them. At the top of each bell, fix a bow of gold-covered wire; on the trees, a little star.

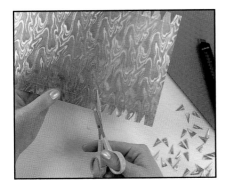

F ill this sleigh with foil wrapped candies for a charming table centrepiece. Apply gold embossed paper to both sides of thick card-board with spray glue and cut a pair of sleighs using the template on page 59. For the base, glue gold paper to both sides of a rectangle of thin cardboard 36cm x 16cm (14$\frac{1}{8}$in x 6$\frac{1}{4}$in).

Mark the broken lines on the sleighs. Score along the base 1.5cm ($\frac{5}{8}$in) from each long edge. Snip away tiny triangles up to the scored lines so that the base will bend easily. Bend the snipped edge backwards at right angles.

Glue the snipped edges between the sleighs along the broken lines and lower, straight edges. Use the template to cut out two flowers in red foil paper and two leaves in green. Glue two leaves under each flower and glue three sequins in the middle. Glue a flower to each side of the sleigh and line it with scrunched up iridescent film.

For a stunning party mask, buy a ready-moulded mask from a stationer's or toy shop. The half-mask shown here is coloured with oil stencil pencils. Start with the pink; apply a little to a piece of waxed paper, then pick it up on the stencil brush. Using a circular motion, cover about half the mask. Repeat with the blue, filling in the gaps and giving the eyes a semblance of eyeliner.

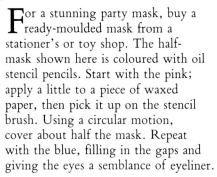

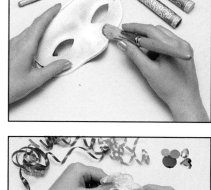

Next take a short length of lace and glue it to the back of the top half of the mask, down to where the elastic is attached. Glue some strands of curling gift wrap ribbon on either side. (Curl the ribbon by running the blunt edge of a pair of scissor along it.) Lastly, glue some large sequins over the tops of the ribbons to hide the ends, and glue another one in the centre of the forehead.

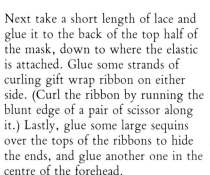

What could be simpler than these crisply-pleated paper fans, trimmed with curling ribbons? To begin, take a strip of printed wrapping paper and pleat it crosswise as shown.

For the black mask, first sew some silver tinsel wire around the edge and around the eyes. Sew on some pearl beads either side, then sew two or three grey or white feathers under the edges for an owlish look.

When you have finished the folding, hold the fan together by stapling it at one end. Cut some strips of gift wrap ribbon and run them along the edge of a ruler, or over a scissors blade, so that they curl.

Slip the ends of the ribbons between the folds of the fan and staple them in place. Finish by fixing a ribbon rosette over the stapled end.

Another beautiful mask to make; this one is lavishly jewelled. Spray glue two pieces of gold cardboard together for extra strength, then use the template on page 59 to cut out the mask. Stick double-sided tape to the top edge on the back of the mask. Cut a strip of iridescent film 50cm x 6cm (20in x 2¼in). Scrunch up one long edge and press onto the tape.

Glue an iridescent plastic flower to the left-hand corner. Glue small glass stones at random to the mask and stick one in the centre of the flower. A pair of tweezers is useful for holding tiny stones. Glue gold plastic leaves around the flower.

Spray a 30cm (12in) length of thin wood dowel gold and bind with narrow giftwrap ribbon. Glue the ends in place. Pull two lengths of giftwrap ribbon between your thumb and finger to coil them. Stick the ribbons to one end of the dowel with sticky tape and use a strong glue to stick the wooden handle behind the mask.

Here's a jaunty majorette's cap that is ideal for a fancy dress party. Cut a strip of coloured cardboard 60cm x 13cm (24in x 5in). Use the template on page 59 to cut out a peak in silver cardboard. On the wrong side, score the peak along the broken lines and make snips in the cardboard to the scored line. Bend the snipped edge upwards.

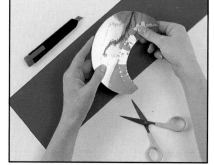

Stick an 18cm (7 in) long strip of double-sided tape in the middle of one long edge of the hat on the wrong side. Overlap the ends of the strip and lightly hold together with masking tape. Press the snipped edge of the peak onto the sticky tape. Remove the masking tape.

Wrap the hat around your head, overlapping the ends, and stick together with double-sided tape. Pleat a rectangle of foil giftwrap and bind the lower edge closed with clear sticky tape, forming a fan. Glue to the front of the hat. Finally, cut out a diamond shape from silver cardboard and glue it over the fan.

These conical hats are so easy to make that you will want to make one for each of your party guests. Cut a 30cm (12in) diameter circle of shiny cardboard for each hat and cut to the centre. Cut a slice out of the circle so that the hat is not too bulky. Overlap the cut edges and glue together.

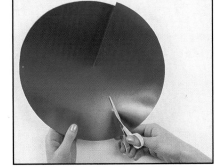

There are many ways to decorate the hats – stick on gold stars or use glitter pens to draw a pattern. Another idea is to spread glue in moon shapes on the hat and then sprinkle on glitter, shaking off the excess.

Make a hole with the points of a pair of scissors each side of the hat and thread with hat elastic. Adjust the elastic to fit under the chin and make a knot behind the holes.

For this you need a large piece of black art paper, 38cm x 39.5cm (15in x 15½in). Mark a 1.5cm (½in) border at one end of the longer side so that you have a 38cm (15in) square. Take a compass, string and a white pencil and mark an arc between two corners. Cut along the arc, spread glue on the border, and use this to join the edges of the cone together.

Use the cone to mark a circle on some black cardboard. Draw another line around the first, about 5cm (2in) from it, then another just 2.5cm (1in) inside the first line. Cut along the inner and outer lines, then make triangular cuts on the inside of the brim. Fold them up and glue them to the inside of the cone. Decorate the hat with gold stars and moons cut from sticky-backed plastic.

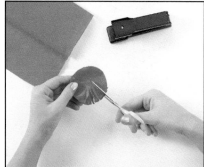

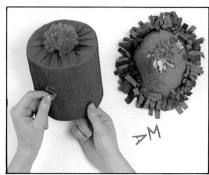

Essential wear at any children's party, these hats even bear the wearer's name. First cut the hats out of lightweight cardboard – a small circle and a rectangular piece for the fez and a semi-circular piece, about 15cm (6in) in diameter, for the conical hat. Glue the sides together to form a tube and a cone, and attach the top circle to the fez with tape. Cover the hats in crepe paper.

To make a tissue pom-pom, fold the tissue to get at least 12 layers, measuring 7cm (3in) square. Using a cup or glass, mark a circle on the paper, and cut it out. Staple the layers together at the centre. Cut strips into the centre, making them about 5mm (¼in) wide at the edge and stopping short of the staple. Fluff up the tissue paper to form a pom-pom.

Make pom-poms for both hats and attach them with glue or double-sided tape. Make a frill for the conical hat by cutting two lengths of crepe paper about 5cm (2in) deep and long enough to go around the edge of the rim. Neatly cut narrow strips about 2cm (¾in) deep on either side of the length to create a fringe. Staple the two layers of 'fringe' onto the rim of the hat.

Cut out paper letters from contrasting-coloured paper and glue names onto the front of each hat.

To make these fake neckties, first trace a pattern from a real necktie, making the top end just under 5cm (2in) across. Then draw a wide border all around this outline. Use the pattern to cut the shape from wrapping paper. Cut an inverted 'V' through the pointed end of the border up to the point of the tie. Fold the borders over, trimming off any excess paper.

Fold under the top of the tie to hide the cut edge. Cut another piece of paper 10cm x 6cm (4in x 2½in). Fold in the long edges to meet, and wrap the band around the top of the tie. Firmly crease the folds on each side.

Now remove this piece and pierce a hole in the middle of each crease. Thread a piece of shirring elastic through the hole as shown; the elastic should fit comfortably around the neck. Knot the ends of the elastic, then glue the 'knot' to the tie, with the cut edges stuck down at the back.

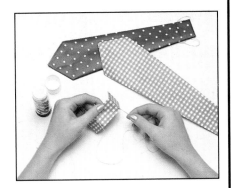

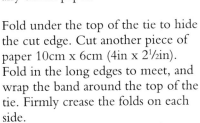

These party bow ties lend a dashing look to a costume. For the flat tie, cut a bow tie shape in thin cardboard. Simply cover the shape with foil, sticky-backed plastic or felt, and attach shirring elastic to the back.

Or make a soft fabric tie by cutting a strip of felt or other material 18cm (7in) square. Fold it in half, right sides together, and sew the long edges together to make a tube. Turn it right side out, and finish the raw edges by turning them in and slip-stitching them.

Cut another strip of material 5cm x 9cm (2in x 3½in). Fold the long edges in to meet at the back and glue them down. Wrap this piece around the middle of the tube and sew it in place at the back, folding in the raw edges to hide them. Sew on shirring elastic for wearing the bow.

If the day outside is gloomy, try brightening the outlook with some 'stained glass window' pictures. These are cut from black art paper and backed with coloured tissue. First cut pieces of art paper 38 by 30cm (15 by 12in). Mark a 3.5cm (1½in) border all the way round. Now draw your design, taking care that it is always connected in some way to the outer border.

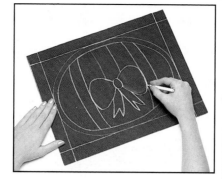

Next cut away any parts of the picture that you want to be coloured, taking care not to detach the black areas from the frame.

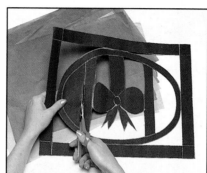

Now glue tissue paper to the back. For your first attempt use just one colour; then as you feel more confident, you can build up pictures using three or more different coloured tissues. When the picture is finished, affix it lightly to the windowpane, then watch what happens when the light shines through it.

These are just as colourful as real balloons, but they won't pop, or even gently expire! Cut out balloon shapes from coloured cardboard or stiff paper, then cover them on one side with spray-on glitter.

Two balloon shapes can be glued together at the edges, or they can all be strung up separately. Tape the balloons to a length of colourful striped ribbon.

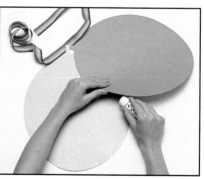

Lastly, use more of the same ribbon to make up some bows, and fix them to the balloons with some double-sided tape.

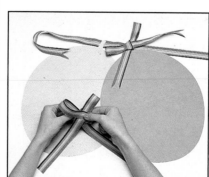

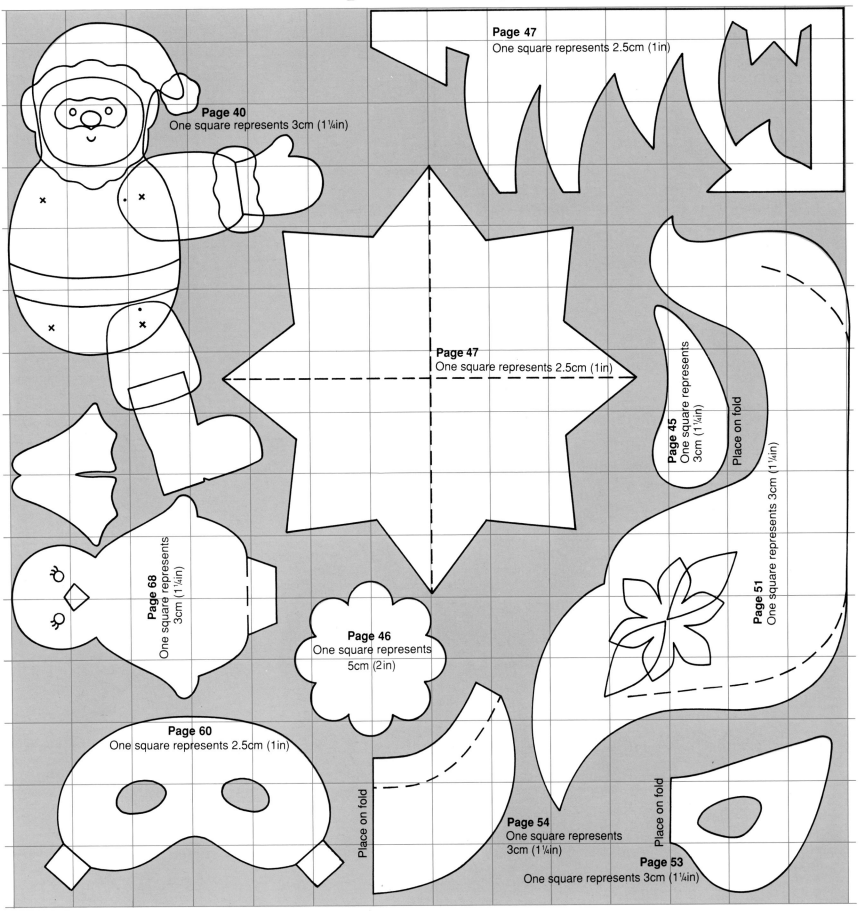

Page 40
One square represents 3cm (1¼in)

Page 47
One square represents 2.5cm (1in)

Page 47
One square represents 2.5cm (1in)

Page 45
One square represents 3cm (1¼in)

Place on fold

Page 51
One square represents 3cm (1¼in)

Page 68
One square represents 3cm (1¼in)

Page 46
One square represents 5cm (2in)

Page 60
One square represents 2.5cm (1in)

Place on fold

Page 54
One square represents 3cm (1¼in)

Place on fold

Page 53
One square represents 3cm (1¼in)

Make that dinner or tea party extra special by creating table decorations in your own style, either to complement your china, the meal itself or simply the occasion. On the following pages you will find a range of ideas to transform your table. As the table centrepiece is often the most important feature we have included a number of beautiful and artistic designs. There are also clever and zany place cards to guide your guests to their seats, crackers for little take-home gifts, co-ordinating place settings as well as novel suggestions for prettying up plain napkins.

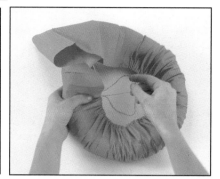

Adorn the New Year dinner table with this attractive centrepiece. Cut a length of magenta crepe paper 120cm x 20cm (48in x 8in). Stick the ends together on the wrong side with clear sticky tape. Place a 25cm (10in) diameter polystyrene ring in the middle and sew the long edges of crepe paper together with a running stitch, enclosing the polystyrene ring. Gather up the seam and fasten off.

Spray five candle holders white and push into the ring, evenly spaced apart. Then drape strings of white pearls and narrow green coiled gift wrapping ribbon around the ring, gluing the ends to the underside.

Stick two rectangles of metallic blue cardboard back to back with spray adhesive and cut out five masks using the template on page 59. Score gently along the fold line of the tabs and bend the tabs backwards. Stick each mask, by the tabs, in front of a candle. Decorate the ring with blue and green star-shaped sequins and silver stars cut from cardboard.

MARZIPAN FRUIT PARCELS  CONE CANDLE STAND

Exquisite marzipan fruits deserve special presentation. Nestling in little tissue 'parcels' and piled into a cake stand, they make a colourful centrepiece. All you need is several different colours of tissue paper and some pinking shears. Instead of marzipan fruits, you could use chocolates or marrons glacés.

Believe it or not, this arrangement is quite simple once you get the hang of folding the cones. You need two colours of foil paper. Cut out lots of boat shapes 16.5cm (6½in) along the top and 12.5 (5in) along the bottom and about 6cm (2½in) deep. Glue one colour to another, back-to-back.

From a double layer of one colour of tissue, cut a 10cm (4in) square. Pinking shears give an attractive serrated edge. From another colour of tissue, also double, cut a smaller square, measuring about 6cm (2½in).

Form each boat into a cone and glue it in place. The first few you make may not look too professional, but it doesn't matter; these can go on the outside of the stand and will be partially covered. You will soon get the hang of folding the cones. Bend the bottoms under; it helps to hold the shape and looks tidier.

Lay the smaller square on top of the larger one. Place the marzipan fruit in the centre and gather the tissue around it. Hold it in place for a few seconds and then let go; the crumpled tissue will retain its rosette shape. Place several of the parcels on a doily-lined glass or china cake stand.

When you have several cones made, start gluing them around the edge of a 20cm- (8in-) diameter silver cake board. Place another two layers inside the first, leaving room for a chunky candle in the middle.

This beautiful cracker is not designed to be pulled but to be taken home as a memento. First take a tube of cardboard and wrap white crepe paper around it. Insert short cardboard tubes into each end, leaving gaps of 5cm (2in) between the main and end sections. Cover the central and end sections on the outside with silver foil paper, and stick pink foil paper to the inside of the end sections.

Wind a length of silver sequin waste around the centre. Next take two strips of pink net and draw a piece of thread through the centre of each to gather it. Tie them at each end with a strip of curling gift wrap ribbon. (Curl the ribbon by running the blunt edge of a pair of scissors along it.)

Finish by decorating the cracker with large sequins and a pink foil heart, or with some other shape if you prefer. If you like, pop a little gift inside — a hand-made chocolate, perhaps, or even a diamond ring!

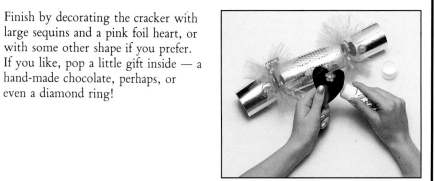

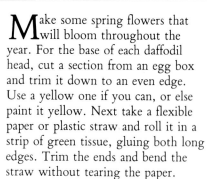

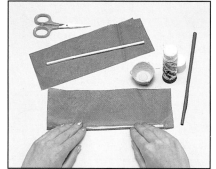

Make some spring flowers that will bloom throughout the year. For the base of each daffodil head, cut a section from an egg box and trim it down to an even edge. Use a yellow one if you can, or else paint it yellow. Next take a flexible paper or plastic straw and roll it in a strip of green tissue, gluing both long edges. Trim the ends and bend the straw without tearing the paper.

Cut out some yellow tissue petals and glue first one row, then a second, around the inside of the egg box base.

Finally, scrunch up a small piece of orange tissue paper and glue it to the centre of the flower.

This collage place card can be made from wrapping paper and scraps of plain stiff paper. Select a gift-wrapping paper with a design that is appropriate to the theme of your party and plain paper in a harmonizing colour. Cut a rectangle of the plain paper about 14 by 9cm (5½ by 3½in) and fold it in half as shown.

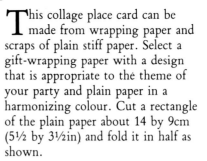

Cut around the shape you have decided to use and stick this to the card with double-sided tape or glue.

Stick additional shapes onto the card as desired. Put double-sided tape onto the back of a small area of the wrapping paper, and cut thin strips with which to make up the names. Peel off the backing and attach the strips to the card to form the letters.

What could be prettier than this profusion of ribbons and flowers? The one shown is pink and white, but you should choose whatever matches your décor. First of all you will need a biscuit or cake tin. Cover the outside with silver foil paper, allowing a little extra at the top to turn over and glue. (This will be easier if you snip down to the tin.) Decorate it with strips of ribbon.

Take a block of florists' foam and cut it to fit inside the tin, using the extra bits to fill in the gaps around it.

Now wire up pieces of gift wrap ribbon, little baubles, strips of crepe paper and silk flowers. Curl the ribbon by running the blunt edge of a pair of scissors along it. Push the wires into the foam, arranging them until the tin is totally full. Use strips of ribbon around the outside, and let them fall over the side of the tin.

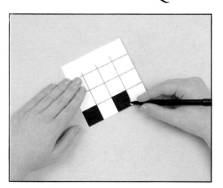

Make cocktail glasses look extra smart with this chequered place card. First cut a 7.5cm (3in) square from a piece of stiff white cardboard. Use a pencil and ruler to mark off 2.5cm (1in) divisions and join these up to form a grid. Colour in alternate squares with a black felt pen to give a chequerboard pattern.

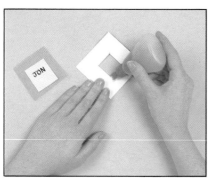

On a 5cm (2in) square of cardboard write the name. Cut out a 6cm (2½in)-square piece of pink net fabric; set it aside. Using a sharp craft knife, cut out the centre of the chequered card to leave a hole 2.5cm (1in) square. Turn the card over and apply some glue around the edges of the hole.

P!ace the piece of net over the card with the name, and hold them together in one hand while positioning the chequered card diagonally over the top. Press firmly to apply the glue to all three surfaces. Leave the card to dry for a few minutes.

This unusual placemat is easily made from cardboard and a wallpaper border. A black and white border has been chosen here, but you can use a colour which co-ordinates with your table setting. Cut a 30cm (12in) square from a sheet of thick cardboard, using a steel rule and craft knife to ensure precision.

Cut the border into four strips, allowing a little extra on each strip for trimming. Apply double-sided tape to the back of each strip, but do not peel off the protective backing yet. Lay two adjacent strips in place; where they meet at the corners, try to match the pattern repeat. Holding one strip on top of the other, cut diagonally across the corner.

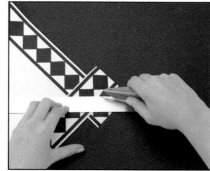

Holding each strip in place along its inner edge, begin to peel back the protective paper from the double-sided tape, as shown. Rub a soft cloth along the border as you peel to stick it in place.

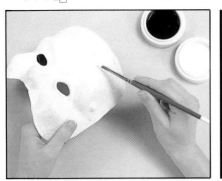

These unusual harlequin masks form the perfect party centre-piece, especially when co-ordinated with a black and white table setting, as shown on page 64. The masks can be bought or home-made from papier mâché. Paint each mask white.

With a pencil draw diagonal lines across the mask to create a grid. Don't worry if the squares are not exactly symmetrical. Paint alternate squares black.

Glue a length of black lace or net around the edge of the mask. Add coloured feathers and ribbons for the finishing touches. Stand the masks back to back so that one is facing each side of the table.

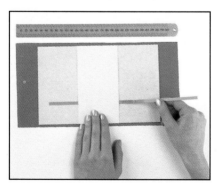

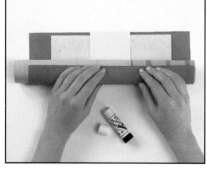

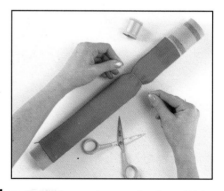

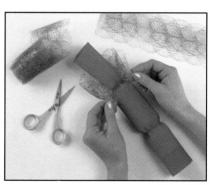

I t is easy and economical to make crackers. Cut crepe paper 32cm x 16cm (12³⁄₄in x 6¹⁄₄in), keeping the grain of the paper parallel with the long sides. Lay a piece of thin writing paper 24cm x 15cm (9¹⁄₂in x 6in) centrally on top. Next cut thin cardboard 15cm x 8cm (6in x 3in) and lay it across the centre. Slip a cracker snap underneath.

Take two cardboard tubes, the sort found inside rolls of kitchen towel, and cut one in half. Lay the long tube on the lower edge of the crepe paper, with the end level with the cardboard edge. Butt a short tube against the long one and roll up tightly. Glue the overlapped edges of paper together with a low-tack adhesive.

Pull the short tube out for 5cm (2in) and tie thread tightly around the cracker between the tubes. Push the tubes together again then remove the short tube. Drop a gift, motto and paper hat inside and pull out the long tube a further 12.5cm (5in) . Tie thread tightly between the tube and cardboard inside the cracker. Untie the threads.

Cut two 25cm (10in) lengths of gold filigree lace – the kind that has a drawstring thread along one edge. Gather up the drawstring and tie the lace around the necks of the cracker. Gently stretch the ends of the cracker to flute the edge. Remove the drawstring from a length of lace and glue around the middle of the cracker. Glue a dried flower head in place to complete.

G old and silver look stunning by candlelight and this festive arrangement will flatter any table setting. To begin, spray a vine garland with gold paint, sprinkle with gold glitter, and leave to dry.

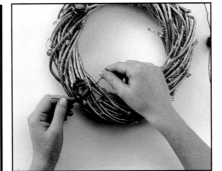

Take three flat-based candle holders and stick florists' fixative putty under each one. Position them evenly-spaced around the garland using florists' wire to secure each holder firmly in place. To make the silver roses – four for each candle – cut strips of silver crepe paper 53cm (21in) long and 9cm (3½in) wide. Fold the strips in half lengthways and tuck the short ends in.

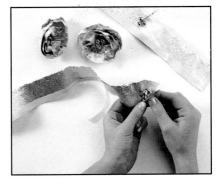

Run a strip of double-sided tape along the lower edge of a folded strip, and place a wired group of small gold balls at one end. Roll the crepe paper around the balls, removing the tape's backing paper as you go and pinching the paper tightly together at the base. When you have finished rolling, crimp the petal edges to curve outwards.

Stick a double-sided adhesive pad to the base of each rose and position four flowers around each candle holder. Cut 23cm (9in) lengths of gold ribbon and fold into double loops. Secure the ends with florists' wire and stick between the roses using adhesive pads. Tease the rose petals and gold loops into shape to hide the holders, and put candles in place.

M iniature holly sprigs give a festive touch to a place card. From thin cardboard cut a rectangle 7.5cm x 10cm (3in x 4in). Gently score across the centre, using a craft knife against a ruler, and fold the card in half. Punch a hole in the lower left side. Make a holly leaf template from thick paper and draw around the edge on to thick green paper (artist's Canson paper is ideal). Cut out.

Score lightly down the centre of each leaf and bend to shape. Bind a bunch of red flower stamens (available from craft shops) together with fine florists' wire and cut in half across the stems to create two bunches. Bind the stamens to the front of the leaves with red florists' tape.

Fold a short length of narrow curling ribbon in half, at a slight angle, and secure fold with a small piece of double-sided tape. Curl the ribbon against a scissor blade and stick to the front of the holly sprig. Write the name on the card and push the holly sprig through the punched hole, securing the stems to the back of the card with a small piece of sticky tape.

T hese cheerful chicks will guide guests to their seats for Easter tea. Use template on page 59 to cut out a chick in lemon coloured cardboard and a beak and feet in orange cardboard. Glue the beak to the chick and draw the eyes with a black felt-tipped pen.

Write the name of your guest with a pencil diagonally on the chick using a letter stencil. Fill in the letters with a felt-tipped pen.

Score along the broken lines on the chick and bend the tab backwards at a right angle. Glue the tab to the chick's feet.

KITE PLACE CARDS

FREE-STYLE PLACE CARD

These colourful place cards are perfect for a children's party. For each kite you will need stiff paper in two colours. From each colour cut two rectangles, each 10 by 15cm (4 by 6in). Draw a line down the centre, then another line at right angles across it, 5cm (2in) from one end. Join up the points, then cut off the four corners; set them aside.

Use two of the corners of the red card to decorate the yellow kite, glueing them in place as shown. Similarly, use two of the leftover pieces of the yellow card to decorate the red kite. Write the name on each kite.

Cut out squares of coloured tissue, allowing three for each kite. On the back of each kite, glue a 40cm (16in) strip of thin ribbon. Pinch the squares of tissue together in the centre and tie the ribbon around them. Cut a small strip of cardboard, fold it in two and glue it to the back of the kite; use this hook to attach the kite to a glass.

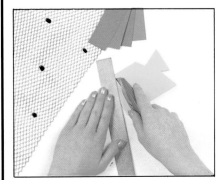

This original place card is simple to make using different colours of stiff paper and scraps of net. First cut a rectangle out of lightweight cardboard, twice the depth of the finished card; fold it in half. Using a craft knife and a steel ruler, cut sections of the card away to create an irregular edge. The cards can be any shape; in fact, it is more fun if they all look a little different.

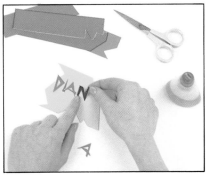

From the coloured paper cut the letters to spell each guest's name. Don't try to cut rounded shapes, as this is more difficult. It may be easier to make some letters from two pieces. For a letter A, for example, cut a V shape, turn it upside down, and add a separate strip for the crossbar. Glue the letters in place.

Cut irregular pieces from a scrap of net, and lightly glue these in place over the name. Place each card on a plate on top of a folded napkin, as shown.

Quick and easy to make, this place mat will brighten up the supper table. Cut a wavy-edged rectangle of blue cardboard 35cm x 25cm (14in x 10in). Cut a row of wavy slits lengthwise across the mat with a craft knife.

This sparkling placemat is an obvious winner for Christmas. First draw a Christmas tree on the reverse (matt) side of a piece of shiny green cardboard. The length should be about 10cm (4in) longer than the diameter of your dinner plate and the width about 20cm (8in) wider. Cut out the mat using a craft knife and a steel ruler.

Cut wavy-edged strips 23cm (9in) long from green cardboard. Weave the first strip in and out of the slits close to one end. Weave in the remaining strips starting each alternate strip at the next slit up.

Add 'ornaments' by sticking tiny baubles to the tips of the tree using strong glue.

On the back, lift up the ends of the strips and glue to the mat. Make a matching coaster from a small wavy-edged square of cardboard.

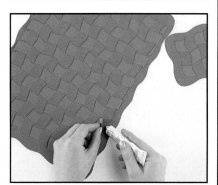

Cut out or buy a star shape to put at the top of the tree. Finally, stick small silver stars over the mat. Or, if you prefer, just scatter the stars freely over the mat, first positioning each mat on the table.

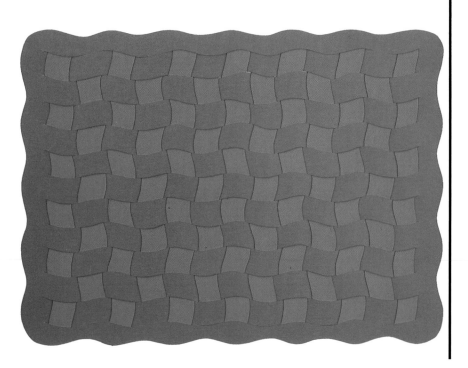

C hristian colours are woven
together to make a matching
table mat and napkin set.
From cartridge paper cut out a

rectangle 37cm x 27cm (14½in x
10½in) and mark a 2.5cm (1in)
border all round. Draw lines 12mm
(½in) apart across the paper. Cut a
piece of sticky-backed velour fabric a
little larger all round and peel off the
backing paper. Lay the rectangle
centrally on top and, using a craft
knife, cut through the drawn lines as
shown. Fold overlapping fabric over
and stick down.

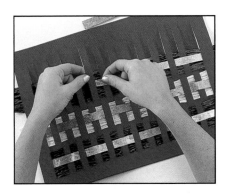

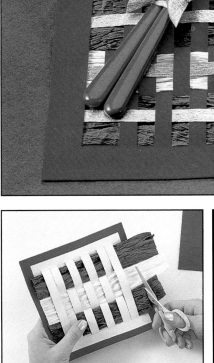

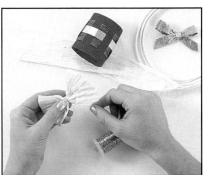

Weave lengths of green and white
paper rope through the cut stripes,
arranging the ribbon so both ends
pass under the border. Fold gold and
silver crepe paper into narrow strips
and weave over the green and white
ribbon. Hold the strips in place with
double-sided tape at both ends. Trim
away the excess paper, then cut a
piece of fabric to cover the back of
the mat.

Cut a coaster mat from cartridge
paper 17cm (6½in) square. Make a
border as for the table mat, and
mark, cover and cut in the same
way. Weave with two lengths of
each colour and cover the back with
sticky-backed fabric as before.

To make the napkin ring, cut a strip
from cartridge paper 17cm x 6.5cm
(6½in x 2½in). Mark out a 12mm
(½in) border and divide into strips
12mm (½in) apart. Cover with
sticky-backed fabric, and cut strips as
before. Weave green ribbon and
silver or gold crepe through the slits
and secure with double-sided tape.
Cut a length of fabric for the
backing and stick in place.

Join the two ends of the ring by
overlapping them and securing with
double-sided tape. Make a bow
shape from white paper ribbon,
binding the centre with fine florists'
wire. Make a small bow shape from
folded gold crepe paper and stick
across the white bow with double-
sided tape. Stick the completed bow
across the join in the napkin ring
using double-sided tape.

Here's a quick and simple way to dress up a plain napkin for afternoon tea. All you need is a square paper doily, preferably in a colour contrasting with the napkin, and a floral motif. Begin by folding the napkin into a triangle.

Here are a couple of ideas for jazzing up ordinary paper napkins. For the blue napkin, cut a star shape from a piece of cardboard — the cardboard must be slightly wider than the folded napkin. Hold the cardboard firmly in place over the napkin and spray silver or gold paint over the area. Let the paint dry for several minutes before you allow anything else to touch it.

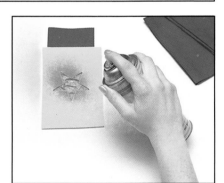

Fold the doily diagonally. To create a 'spine' to allow for the thickness of the napkin, unfold the doily and make another crease about 1cm (³⁄₈in) from the first fold.

The white napkins have a design stencilled on them with oil-based stencil crayons. You can buy these separately or in packs, with ready-cut stencils. Choose your design, then place it over the area you want to stencil — in this case the corner of the napkin. Rub the crayon over a spare area of stencil, then take the colour up onto the brush and paint it over the stencil, in a circular motion.

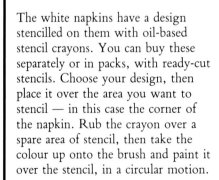

Cut out a Victorian scrap or other floral motif and glue it to the centre of the smaller (top) side of the doily. Insert the napkin.

Use the brush only over the parts you wish to show up in that colour. Now switch to the next colour. It is best to use a different brush for each colour if you want clear colour definition.

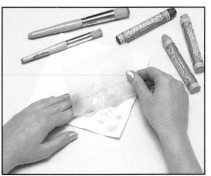

GIFT WRAPPING
& GREETING CARDS

One form of paper craft that most of us have practised
for years, probably without realizing it, is gift wrapping. Yet,
as we all know, it is so easy to run out of ideas. Well, no more. In this
section you will find over 80 imaginative ways to wrap gifts and add those all
important finishing touches. There are ideas for making your own attractive wrapping
papers, gift boxes and bags, hints on how to wrap a variety of different
shaped gifts, a wide and colourful range of pom-poms, rosettes and
unusual decorations, and some very pretty gift tags.

If you want to be really original, you can even make
your own greeting cards. The final chapter in this section
contains over 60 fun ideas for creating cards for all occassions; so
whether you wish to say 'Happy Birthday', 'Merry Christmas', 'Bon Voyage' or simply
ask someone to a party, you'll find just the card to suit you. And although
it's easy enough to make a base card out of lightweight coloured cardboard,
it's easier still to buy a 'card blank' from the
wide range now available in craft shops.

The huge selection of gift wraps on the market should give you plenty of scope for covering your presents. But you don't have to use a ready-made gift wrap — for real individuality and style, you can make your own. The following pages will give you plenty of ideas. For example, what about stencilling your own design, creating a collage, or printing a pattern with a humble potato?

And once you have your wrapping paper, there are lots of tips on how to use it properly, such as how to wrap a cylindrical gift neatly; or what to do with a spherical shape. For more, just read on.

There's no excuse for an unimaginatively wrapped present with such a spectacular range of gift wrap available. Choose from plain, matt, shiny, pastel or bold colours, glossy or glittery designs, to make the most of your gift.

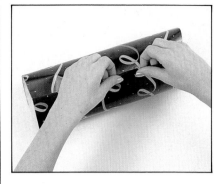

When wrapping a cylinder, avoid using very thick or textured paper as it will be difficult to fold neatly. Cut the paper longer than the cylinder, allowing for extra paper at each end to cover half the cylinder's diameter, and just wider than the gift's circumference. Roll the paper around the parcel and secure with a little tape.

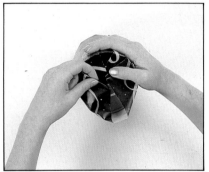

Begin folding the ends of the paper in a series of small triangles as shown here. Continue around the whole circumference, making sure that the 'triangles' are neatly folded into the centre.

Use a single piece of tape at the centre to fix all the folds in place. If the finished folds are not even, you could cheat a little by sticking a circle of matching gift wrap over each end of the cylinder.

Wrapping square or rectangular presents isn't difficult — but perhaps your technique needs brushing up. Wrap the gift wrap tightly around the box. You can simply stick down the free edge with tape or, for a smarter effect, fold over the top edge of the paper and stick double-sided tape underneath it, leaving a neat fold visible at the join.

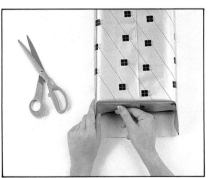

If your paper has a linear design, try to align the design so that the join is not too obvious. Fold the joined section of paper down over the end of the box to make a flap; crease the fold neatly. Trim off any excess paper so there is no unnecessary bulk.

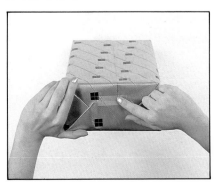

Crease the side flaps firmly, and fold them over the ends of the gift. Smoothing your hand along the side of the box and round on to the end ensures that each flap fits tightly. Fold up the remaining triangular flap, pulling it firmly along the edge of the box, and stick down; use invisible tape (its matt surface is scarcely discernible) or double-sided for the best results.

The usual method of wrapping a sphere is to gather the paper around the gift and bunch it all together at the top. Here is a more stylish method. Put your circular gift in the centre of a square of paper, checking that the two sides of paper just meet at the top when wrapped around the gift. Cut off the corners of the square to form a circle of paper.

Bring one section of the paper to the top of the gift and begin to pleat it to fit the object as shown. The paper pleats at the top of the gift will end up at more or less the same point; hold them in place every three or four pleats with a tiny piece of sticky tape.

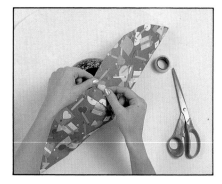

Continue pleating neatly and tightly all the way round the circle. It isn't as complicated or as time-consuming as it sounds once you've got the knack! When you have finished, the pile of pleats on top of the gift should look small and neat. Then you can either cover them with a small circle of paper stuck in place or, more attractively, add a bunch of colourful ribbons.

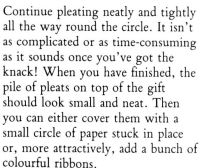

Wrapping awkwardly-shaped presents is just that — awkward. The gift wrap always looks creased and untidy around the angles of the gift. The solution is not to use paper — instead, use brightly-coloured cellophane which doesn't crumple. Cut a square of cellophane a great deal larger than your gift.

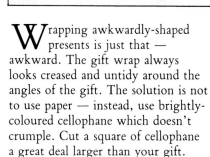

Gather the cellophane up and tie it into a bunch above the present. Fan out the excess and add some curled ribbon as a finishing touch. Alternatively, if your gift is cylindrical, roll it in cellophane somewhat longer than the parcel and gather the ends with ribbon.

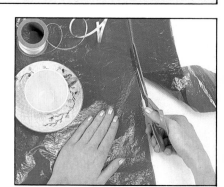

Stylish, expensive-looking wrapping paper can be achieved very quickly with this method of spray stencilling. Choose some plain coloured paper for a base, and make your stencils from plain cardboard or paper. Cut the stencils into squares of two different sizes; alternatively you could use any kind of basic shape — stars, circles or whatever.

Lay some of the shapes in a random pattern across the plain paper, holding them in place with a spot of Plasticine or modelling clay. Cover the whole paper with paint spray. Use car paint or craft spray paint, but do carry it out in a well-ventilated room.

Once the paint is dry take off the sprayed squares and put a new random pattern of fresh squares across the paper. Overlap some of the original squares with the new ones to create interesting effects, then spray the entire sheet with a second colour of paint. Remove the squares and leave the wrapping paper to dry before using it.

Stencilling is great fun to do — and so easy. Design a simple motif then make a trace of it. With a soft pencil, scribble over the back of the trace and put the tracing paper face up on stencil cardboard. Draw round the design again, pressing hard so that the lines are transferred on to the cardboard beneath. Repeat the motif several times and cut out the shapes with a craft knife.

Position the cut-out stencil on plain paper, and either hold it or use masking tape to keep it in place. Mix up some poster paint, keeping the consistency quite thick. Apply the paint through the stencil, using a stiff brush. When you have finished a row of motifs, lift the stencil carefully and blot it on newspaper so that it is ready to use again. Leave the design to dry.

Keep repeating the process until you have covered enough paper to wrap your gift. To help you keep the spacing even between each run of motifs, add some 'markers' to the stencil. Cut half a motif at the end of the run and another one above the run to mark the position of the next row. Paint the markers along with the other motifs, then use this image for re-positioning the next row.

DESIGN WITH A SPONGE

SPATTER PATTERNS

A ll kinds of effects can be achieved with a sponge and some paint. You'll need a piece of natural sponge as man-made sponge doesn't produce the right effect. Choose some plain paper and mix up some poster paint to a fairly runny consistency. Test the paint on a spare piece of paper until you're happy with the colour.

Dab the sponge into the paint and pat it evenly over the paper. The sponge should hold sufficient paint for about four 'dabs' before you need to dip it into the paint again. You'll need to mix up a lot of paint as the sponge absorbs a considerable amount.

Rinse the sponge out well and squeeze dry. When the paper has dried, repeat the process with another colour — you can use as many colours as you wish. Match the ribbon to one of the colours; see page 31 for instructions on how to create the ribbon trim shown here.

T his method makes striking wrapping paper — with apologies to artist Jackson Pollock! Creating the pattern is great fun, but rather messy; cover your work area well with an old cloth or waste paper before you start. Begin by mixing up two or more colours in fairly runny poster paint.

Load a paintbrush with colour, and, with a flicking movement, shake it across the sheet of paper. Repeat several times at various angles to cover the paper. Wait for the paint to dry.

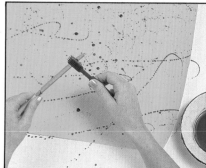

Dip an old toothbrush in another colour paint, avoiding getting the brush too full of liquid. Rub the toothbrush across the blade of a knife to cause the paint to spatter over the paper. Repeat until the spattering is as dense as you like.

FLORAL COLLAGE

Take a tip for decorating your gift from the Victorians, who made glorious scrapbooks and pictures using the art of collage. Collage looks best on plain paper; humble brown paper works admirably. Collect some flower catalogues and you're ready to begin.

From the illustrations of flowers, cut out as many shapes, sizes and colours as you like. Cut fairly accurately around the outline of each flower — it's fiddly, but worth it.

Lay the cut-out flowers on the wrapped parcel. Arrange the pictures in an attractive pattern, then stick them in place with glue. Finally, cut out individual flower petals to form the recipient's name. You can vary this idea by making a collage of a favourite cartoon character for a child or a current pop idol for a teenager.

WHAT'S IN A NAME?

The ultimate in personalized gift wrapping — write the recipient's name all over it! Choose a plain wrapping paper, and three contrasting felt-tipped pens. Hold the pens together in a row and secure them with sticky tape. Before applying the tape, you must ensure the pens are level so that each pen writes with ease.

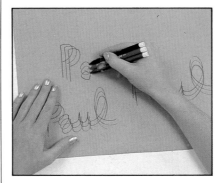

Write the recipient's name randomly across the page in a rounded, flamboyant style. You could vary the effect by grouping the pens in a cluster, rather than a row, or using four or even five pens. Another variation would be to write the name smaller in ordered columns, to give a striped effect.

When you've finished covering the paper with the name, continue the three-tone theme of the gift by tying it up with three ribbons which match the colours of the pens. No one could mistake who this present is for!

A GIFT IN A GIFT

PAPER DUET

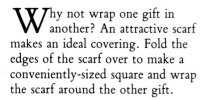

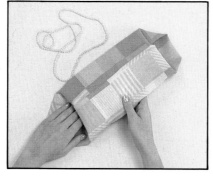

Why not wrap one gift in another? An attractive scarf makes an ideal covering. Fold the edges of the scarf over to make a conveniently-sized square and wrap the scarf around the other gift.

Tuck the top layer of each end of the scarf under the other present as shown, then fold up the end flaps. Use a ribbon or string of beads to hold the flaps in place. Alternatively, a couple of pretty handkerchiefs make a good wrapping for a small gift such as soap. Gather the hankies around the gift and secure in a bunch with a length of lace.

It is very annoying if the gift wrap you have bought is just too small to cover your present. The answer is to use two pieces of contrasting paper — the result can be very chic! Wrap your gift with one of the pieces of paper, using a strip of scrap paper to protect the gift from the tape. Fold in the ends neatly.

Cut the contrasting gift wrap into a strip the exact width of your parcel, long enough to cover the back and both ends plus two flaps. Use this strip to hide the uncovered back of the gift and fold it over the two ends. Make two flaps on the front of the parcel as shown and secure with double-sided tape. Alternatively, wrap each end of the parcel in different paper, hiding the join with a ribbon.

Employ a humble potato to create simple yet beautiful designs. Begin by cutting a large potato in half and draw a simple design on it. Use a sharp knife or craft knife to sculp the potato, leaving the design raised from the surface.

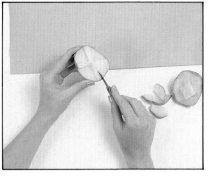

To ensure a regular print, draw a grid lightly in pencil on a sheet of plain paper. Then mix up fairly thick poster paint and apply it to the potato-cut with a paintbrush. Print the design in the middle of each square of the grid. You should be able to do two or three prints before the colour fades and needs replenishing.

Glittering wrapping paper is always glamorous, and with glitter available in such a variety of colours your creativity need know no bounds! Spread out a sheet of plain coloured paper and, using a bottle of glue with a fine nozzle, draw a series of simple patterns across it.

Cover the whole sheet with one design. Cut another design on another potato half; repeat the whole process, this time printing on the cross of the grid. When the paint is thoroughly dry, rub out the grid lines still visible and wrap up your present.

Sprinkle a line of glitter across the paper. Tip up the sheet and gently shake all the glitter from one side of the paper to the other, across the glued designs, making sure that all the patterns have been well covered. Tip the excess glitter off the page on to a sheet of newspaper; the glitter can then be used again.

Now use the glue to make more designs and coat these in glitter of a different colour. Localize the sprinkling of the glitter over the new patterns to be covered and leave to dry. Tip off the excess glitter and return it to its container.

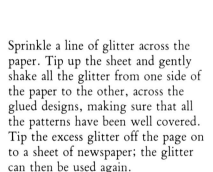

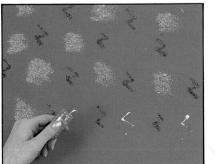

I f the present you've bought is an awkward shape, why waste time and energy trying to wrap it up neatly? Make a box – or a bag – and just pop your gift inside. No more fuss or effort! And the person who receives your gift gets a bonus, since he or she can use the box or bag again afterwards.

On the following pages, there are instructions for making a number of different cardboard boxes, and two kinds of fabric bags. The patterns for the boxes can be found on pages 160–161, and by scaling them up or down you can make a box of any size you like.

Why not try your hand at making a container from this smart selection of gift boxes and bags. They are totally professional in finish, yet remarkably straightforward to make.

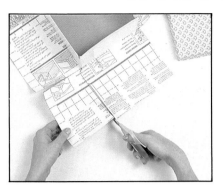

When re-covered in plastic, a shoe box makes a great container for a present. Put the box in the centre of a piece of self-adhesive plastic and draw around it. Then draw around the shape of the sides and ends of the box so you end up with a diagram of the 'exploded' box. Allow extra plastic all round for overlaps. Cut out the pattern you have just created.

Peel the backing off the plastic and position the box carefully in the middle of the covering. Smooth the rest of the plastic up over the box, starting with the ends. Wrap the small overlap around the corners as shown.

Smooth the plastic up over the sides, trimming off the edges to make the pieces the exact size of the sides. Fold over the overlaps around the rim. Cover the lid in the same way. For complete co-ordination, you could cover the inside of the box to match. Alternatively, you could line the box with co-ordinating tissue paper or net.

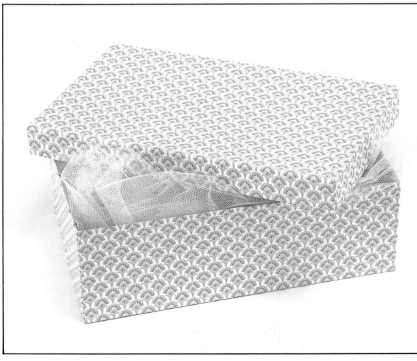

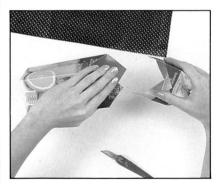

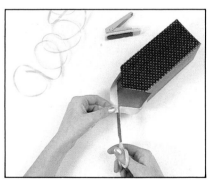

A handy gift container, ideal for home-made sweets, can be made from a well-washed juice carton. Draw V-shapes in each side of the carton. These should be inverted on two opposite sides, and pointing towards the top of the carton on the other two sides. Cut cleanly along the drawn lines with a craft knife as shown.

Cover the carton with gift wrap; adhesive in spray form achieves the best results. Make sure the join lies neatly down one corner of the box. Trim the overlap at the top of the carton so that it is even and fold the paper over the edges, taking care that the corners are neat. Punch a hole at the apex of both the pointed sides and thread ribbon through.

This cube-shaped box is ideal for containing any kind of gift and it can be made to any size. Measure out the shape of the box on to thin cardboard, following the template on page 160. It's very important that all the squares are exactly the same size and that all the angles are right angles. Cut out the shape, and score along the fold lines – the back of a craft knife is useful for doing this.

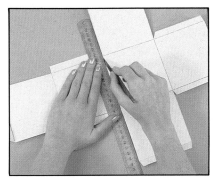

Bend the card carefully along the score lines, making a neat crease along each fold. Crease the flaps on the lid and base and fold the four sides into the shape of the box.

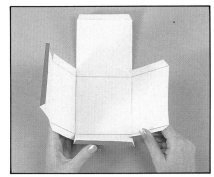

Stick the side flap to its opposite side as shown. You can glue this, or alternatively, use double-sided tape. Fold in the base flap – it should fit precisely and thus give the box rigidity. Finally close the lid flap.

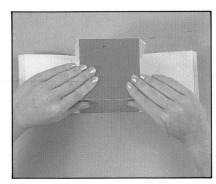

Making a box from scratch can be a little complicated, so why not start with an empty cereal packet? Take your cereal packet and carefully open it out flat. Separating the joins needs care – if necessary slide a knife between the seams to part the glue, rather than tear the packet.

Draw the box you want, using the template on page 160 as a reference. Make sure the lid measures the same as the width of the side panels. Cut out the new shape with a pair of scissors, and cover it with your chosen gift wrap. Spray adhesive is best, since this gives a very smooth finish, however glue in a stick form will do. When the glue has dried, cut neatly around the cardboard shape.

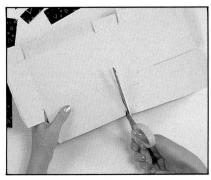

Score along the new fold lines of the box using the back of a craft knife or the blunt edge of a pair of scissors. Fold the box into shape. Stick the side flap in place as shown; you can use double-sided tape or glue. Fix the two flaps on the bottom (either glue or tape them). Put in some shredded tissue as padding, slot in your gift and tuck the lid neatly into place.

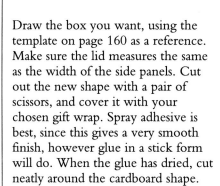

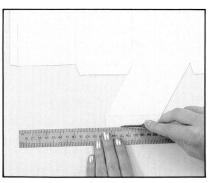

A variation on the cube gives this box an unusual diamond shape. Draw the template on page 160 on to thin coloured cardboard. Check that all the sides are the same size, and that their angles measure 90°; the angles of the lid and base should measure about 60° and 120°. Cut out the shape with a craft knife.

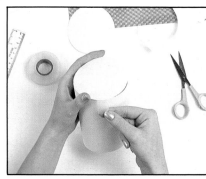

A cylindrical box looks much more difficult to make than it is. Wrap a piece of thin cardboard around the gift to determine the measurement of the box. Cut out the cardboard, roll it up and stick down the edge with a length of tape. Draw and cut out a circular base, and a slightly larger circle for the lid. Attach the base with small bits of tape.

Score along the fold lines on the sides and flaps of the box with the back of a craft knife or the blunt edge of a pair of scissors. Fold the scored edges over, making sure that they are well creased for a crisp shape.

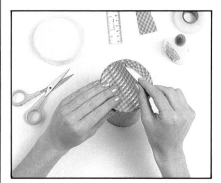

Cut a strip of cardboard slightly longer than the circumference of the cylinder. To make the lid, stick the edge of the strip to the edge of the circle with tape. Next, spread glue on some gift wrap and roll the cylinder in it. Cut the paper to fit, allowing an overlap each end. Tuck the overlap into the open end; secure. Fold the base overlap in a series of small triangles and stick to the base.

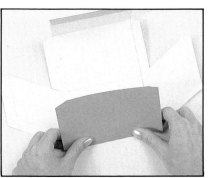

Fit the box together, sticking down the side flap with glue or double-sided tape. Fold in the base and the lid; it is the shape of these which converts the box from being an ordinary cube into the more exotic diamond shape.

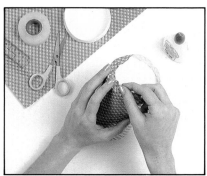

Draw a circle of gift wrap slightly smaller than the base. Cut it out and glue in position, hiding all the folds and bits of tape. Cover the lid in the same way. If you like, you can punch two holes in each side of the container and thread through short lengths of decorative braid.

S mart handles give this box style; they are also the mechanism for closing it. Use coloured cardboard for the box; if you try to cover the box pattern with gift wrap it will lift off. Copy the template on page 161, scaling it up or down if you wish. Use a compass to draw the handles. Cut out the shape with a craft knife, taking great care with the handles and their slots.

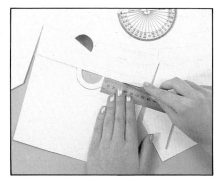

Score along all the fold lines using the back of a craft knife; crease them well. Fold the carton into shape, and stick down the side flap with double sided tape or glue. Fold the base down, pushing the flap inside the box to secure it.

T his attractive and unusual bag will add prestige to any present. Draw the template featured on page 160 on to a sheet of thin cardboard with the aid of a compass and a protractor; use a pencil as some of the design will need to be erased later. Cut out the circle and score along the lines of the 'star' and the central octagon with a sharp edge – the back of a craft knife will do.

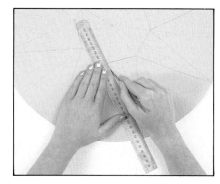

Close the first two flaps of the lid, folding the handles up to fit. Pinch the handles together and fold the two top flaps of the lid over them, fitting the handles through the slots.

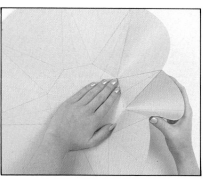

Take care not to overscore along the intersections of the lines, as the cardboard could eventually tear. Rub out any line not scored. Bend along the edges of the octagon, being careful not to crease the sides. Then fold along the arms of the 'star', to form a series of triangles (these will come together to form the container for your gift).

Folding the box needs patience, but it's not as complicated as it looks! When the folding is complete, punch holes either side of the top of each triangle (see the template) and thread the ribbon through the holes as shown. Arrange the curved edges so that they radiate out from the centre. You can make the bag any size you want; as a guide, though, ours had a diameter of 40cm (16in).

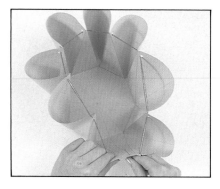

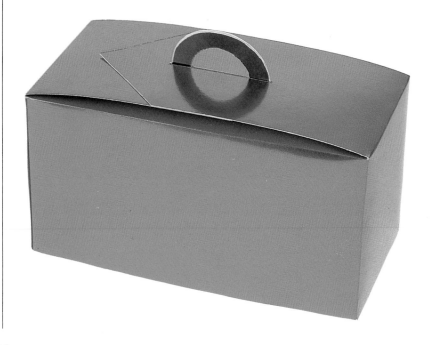

TRIANGULAR TREAT

A plant is a notoriously difficult item to wrap; here's a smart solution. Measure an equilateral triangle on some coloured cardboard. The length of each side should be twice the height of the plant; use a protractor to ensure all the angles measure 60°.

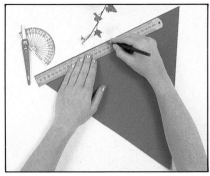

Divide each of the three sides of the triangle in half. Join all the half marks together to form an inner equilateral triangle; this will form the base. Bend the card along a ruler at each inner line as shown and bring up the sides to form a three-dimensional triangle. Punch a hole in each apex and thread ribbon through to close the parcel; double length ribbon gives a pretty finishing touch.

SMART SACHETS

These sachets are ideal for ties, soaps, scarves, jewellery, hankies, socks and so forth. On to thin cardboard, trace the template on page 161. It's probably more interesting to cover the shape with gift wrap as shown here, but you can use plain cardboard if you wish. If using gift wrap, cut out the shape and paste it on to your chosen wrapping paper.

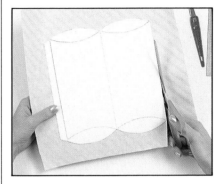

Cut out the covered shape. Then score well along the curved lines of the ellipses which will form the overlapping ends of the packet. Use the back of a craft knife or the blunt side of a pair of scissors to make the score marks.

Stick the side flaps together with either double-sided tape or glue. Fold in the ends; if you've scored the lines sufficiently they should pop in easily with just a little guidance. They can be re-opened with no difficulty but make sure the covering gift wrap doesn't begin to lift off the cardboard.

This method is best suited to a small box as the end result is not particularly strong. From thin cardboard, cut out a cross-shaped piece as shown, made up of four sides and a base, all the same size and all absolutely square. The lid will also be a square measuring 5mm (¼in) larger than the base, with sides about 2cm (¾in) deep.

These rigid little boxes are ideal for presenting jewellery but you can make them to fit anything you like. Choose thin cardboard, either in the colour you want the finished box to be, or white so that you can cover it later with gift wrap. Measure out the template on page 161. The size of the triangular sides doesn't matter, as long as they are all the same, and the base is a true square.

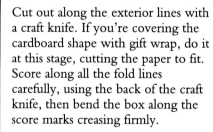

Cut out along the exterior lines with a craft knife. If you're covering the cardboard shape with gift wrap, do it at this stage, cutting the paper to fit. Score along all the fold lines carefully, using the back of the craft knife, then bend the box along the score marks creasing firmly.

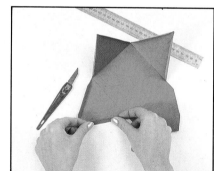

Paste both shapes on to gift wrap and when dry cut off the gift wrap around the box and lid, leaving a small turning or flap around each edge. Fold in the flap on the left of each side of the box and glue it down as shown. Score along the edges of what will be the base, to form fold lines for the sides of the box.

Bend the sides upwards. Put glue on the patterned side of the flaps of gift wrap left unfolded on each side; stick these flaps inside the box to the adjacent sides as illustrated. Crease down the sides firmly and leave to dry. Finally, fold in and glue the top lip. Treat the lid in exactly the same way.

Punch holes in each apex and fold the box into its pyramidal shape. Thread the ribbon in and out of the four holes and, making sure all the side-folds are tucked inside the box, tie the loose ends together with a bow.

This small narrow box would be ideal for giving someone a watch or a piece of jewellery – unless, of course, you make it bigger! Trace off the template on page 161 on to thin cardboard. Cut it out, and either cover it in gift wrap or, if you like the colour of the cardboard, just leave it plain.

Cut around the template with small sharp scissors to trim away the excess gift wrap; take extra care with the slots and handles. Then score along all the fold lines, using the back of the craft knife or the blunt edge of the scissors.

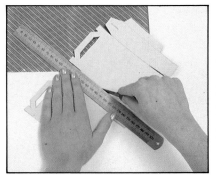

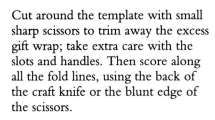

Crease all the folds properly. Fold the box into shape and stick the side flap to the inside of the opposite side. Close the top section, being sure to fold the lid sections upright as shown, halfway across at the point where the two handles meet. Fold over the end flaps and slot them in position to close the box. Finally close the base.

Gift bags are very useful as containers for awkwardly-shaped presents and they can be made to any size. Find something with the required dimensions of the finished bag to serve as a mould – a pile of books should suffice. Choose a good quality, strong gift wrap for making the bag. Cut a strip of gift wrap long enough to wrap round the 'mould' and fold over the top edge.

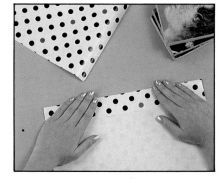

Wrap the paper round the mould; glue or use double-sided tape to join the seam at the back. Fold over the end flaps in the usual way of wrapping any parcel to make the base of the bag; be sure to attach sufficient tape to make the base strong.

Slip the mould out. Fold in the sides of the bag, creasing them in half at the top; fold the base up over the back of the bag. Punch two holes, spaced apart, at the top of the front and back of the bag as shown. Thread through a length of cord to form a handle; knot each end inside the bag. Repeat on the other side. Alternatively, you could thread the bag with ribbons.

An origami envelope is a novel way to present a card or a gift token. You need an accurate square of any kind of paper. We cut a piece of paper 33cm (13in) square. Take your square, fold a diagonal line across and crease. Fold again in the opposite direction, do not crease but mark centre with a light press.

Open up and then fold corner up to the centre mark on your first diagonal crease. Smooth crease firmly with your fingers.

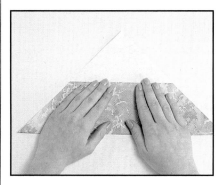

Fold again on original diagonal crease. Smooth down firmly with both hands.

Measure your folded card generously and draw out measurement onto a large piece of paper. Mark centre with a cross. Measure distance from cross to top of card and add on same again, plus 1cm (³⁄₈in) for overlap, to form apex of top flap. Repeat for bottom, then side flaps but exclude extra for overlap. Rule flaps in pencil.

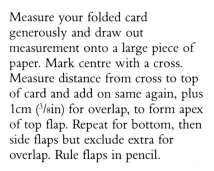

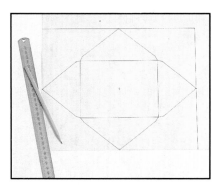

Divide this fold into three and fold right-hand point over to meet first third, and left-hand point to meet new side fold. Smooth up side creases firmly. Fold back front point so that it meets left-hand fold and crease firmly.

Cut out your envelope, score (if using card) and fold in side flaps. Fold in bottom flap and glue to side flaps using a glue pen. Glue down top flap when you have written your card.

Open up this triangle, so that it becomes a diamond, into which the top flap will tuck to close the envelope.

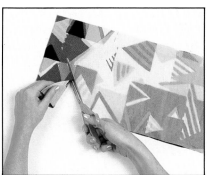

A flat gift can be slipped into this pretty and useful fabric envelope. Make a paper pattern measuring about 5cm (2in) wider than your gift and two and a half times its depth, cutting a shallow V-shape at one end for the flap. Fold your fabric in half and position the paper pattern with the straight edge opposite the pointed end on the fold. Pin it on and cut the fabric out.

With right sides of the fabric together, pin and sew around the edges, leaving a small opening of about 7.5cm (3in); this is to enable the bag to be turned inside out. Turn the bag and press it. Then sew up the gap which was left. You can of course sew all this by hand if you prefer.

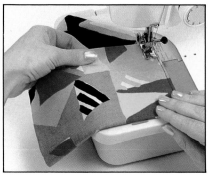

Fold the strip into an envelope shape, with the pointed flap at the top. Pin up the edges carefully and sew them in position with a double row of stitching as shown. Sew a length of ribbon on to the back of the bag with a couple of smaller stitches, pop in the present and tie the ribbon in a bow at the front.

A few pretty soaps are a doubly welcome gift when wrapped in one of these pretty fabric draw-string bags. Cut a strip of cotton fabric about 5cm (2in) wider than you want the finished bag to be, and about 10cm (4in) longer. Turn in about 5cm (2in) at the top of each edge and run a double line of stitching along it to form a channel for the draw-strings.

Pin the side seams with the right sides of the fabric together, making sure the tops of both sides match. Sew the seams, leaving a gap at each end of the draw-string channel. If you don't have a sewing machine, the sewing can be done easily by hand.

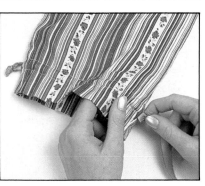

Turn the bag right side out and press it. Get some ribbon four times longer than the width of the bag and cut it in half. Attach a safety pin to the end of one half; thread it and the ribbon through the channels around the top of the bag so that both ends come out of one side. Knot the ends. Thread the other ribbon through both channels too, so the ends come from the other side; knot these too.

Usually it's easy to guess the contents of a parcel that is a recognisable shape, but not if you disguise it! In this section, a bottle turns into a pencil, a record becomes a kite, a cube is given interest as a dice and a round gift turns into a birthday cake.

The exciting ideas on the following pages are good not only for covering awkward shapes or disguising 'obvious' presents, such as bottles, books and records; they also provide novel ideas for wrapping presents for children. Gift wrapping for special occasions, such as Valentine's Day and Christmas, calls for extra inspiration; try the ideas on pages 97 and 99 to start you off.

Whether your present is for Christmas, Valentine's Day or a christening, you can have great fun wrapping it to match the occasion. Or how about disguising it as a birthday cake or a domino? No one will ever guess what's inside.

A romantic padded heart containing a little gift is perfect to give on Valentine's Day! Cut out two heart shapes from cardboard, one about 4cm (1½in) larger all round than the other. From red lining fabric, cut out a heart shape a little bigger than the larger heart. Take a gift box, wrap it in cotton wool (absorbent cotton) and place it on top of the smaller heart.

When there's enough padding, cover the heart in the red lining, stretching it over the heart shape and sticking it firmly in position on the back with plenty of tape. You'll need to snip the fabric around the inverted point of the heart so that the fabric can open out to fit properly.

Cover the larger heart in white tissue paper, otherwise the brown surface may show through the lacey doily. Cut off a frill of about 5cm (2in) from the edge of four or five doilies, and pleat them up around the edge of the large heart, fixing them with tape as shown. When the whole heart has been edged like this, apply some strong glue to the middle and place the padded heart in position.

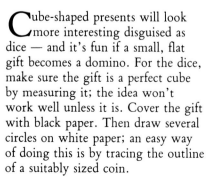

Cube-shaped presents will look more interesting disguised as dice — and it's fun if a small, flat gift becomes a domino. For the dice, make sure the gift is a perfect cube by measuring it; the idea won't work well unless it is. Cover the gift with black paper. Then draw several circles on white paper; an easy way of doing this is by tracing the outline of a suitably sized coin.

Cut out the circles carefully and lay them on the box; glue them in place. Look at a real dice to get the juxtaposition of the sides correct. The domino can be treated in the same way.

T his heart of woven paper can hold a Valentine's Day gift. Lightweight paper in contrasting colours gives the best effect. Cut a strip of paper 25cm by 10cm (10in by 4in) and draw the template on page 161 on to it. Cut the shape out and fold it in half. Then cut the two slits as indicated on the template. Repeat with another strip of paper in a different colour.

Hold a section of the heart in each hand, as shown, with the strips pointing upwards. Weave the two sections together, starting with the two inner strips. You need to open out each strip to slot the other strip through it, as illustrated.

Continue doing this until all the strips are interwoven. It is fairly fiddly but does work; it's clear at this stage why you need lightweight but strong paper! The finished item will open out like a basket, so that it can hold small gifts. The basket would also be very pretty made in felt.

D isguise a bottle as a pencil and keep the recipient guessing! Make a cylinder, about 5cm (2in) shorter than the bottle, from light cardboard, join the sides with tape. Draw a third section of a circle – about 7.5cm (3in) radius – on pale cardboard and cut it out. Roll it in to a cone shape, running the flat edge of a pair of scissors along it to help it curl. Tape in place.

Make a small cone for the lead of the pencil and glue it on to the larger cone. Attach several lengths of sticky tape to the inside edge of the cone and, putting your arm inside the cylinder, stick the tape down to hold the cone in position. Fit the pencil over the bottle and secure with two strips of tape across the bottom.

W hat fun for a child to see Frosty and know that the snowman's hiding a gift! Wrap up a cylindrical gift in paper to form the body of the snowman. Crush newspaper into a shape for the head and stick it on top of the gift. Cover the body with cotton wool (absorbent cotton), sticking it on with dabs of glue. Create a face from bits of paper and stick in place.

For the hat you need a strip of cardboard, plus a circle big enough to make the brim. Draw an inner circle in the brim, the diameter of Frosty's head; cut it out to form the 'lid' of the hat. Roll the strip of cardboard up to form the crown of the hat; stick it in place with tape.

Stick on the top of the hat, then attach the brim, putting strips of tape inside the crown. Paint the hat with black poster paint; it'll need two or three coats. Wrap around the red ribbon to form a cheery hat-band and put it on Frosty's head. Fray the ends of some patterned ribbon to form a scarf and tie it firmly in place.

B righten up a dull-looking, flat gift by turning it into a playing card. Wrap the present in plain white paper. Make a template for the spade by folding a piece of paper in half and drawing half the outline against the fold; this way the design will be symmetrical. Trace around the template on to black paper and cut the shape out. Stick the spade in the centre of the 'card'.

Cut two small spades for the corner designs. Then, using a ruler, draw an 'A' in two of the corners, being careful to make them both the same. Glue the small spades underneath. Cut a piece of patterned paper – smaller than the card – and stick it on the back. You could vary the idea by making the King or Queen of Hearts for your husband or wife, or the ten of clubs for a ten-year-old.

Make a small present look that extra bit special — and that extra bit bigger! Wrap the gift into a ball shape, then cut a strip of paper about three times the width of the gift and long enough to form loops on each side of it. Fold the edges over. Gather small pleats at each end, securing them with sticky tape. Pinch-pleat four gathers in the middle of the strip and secure.

For the trailing sections of the bow, cut a five-sided piece of paper as shown. Fold over the edges in to the centre at the back and secure with tape. Gather pinch pleats at one end and secure. At the other end cut out a V-shaped section to form a nicely-shaped tail. Repeat the procedure a second time.

Turn the pleated ends of the long strip to the middle to form the loops, and secure with double-sided tape. Stick the tails under the bow with more tape. Finally, put double-sided tape over the join on top of the bow and stick the gift in position. Puff out the loops so they look nice and full.

Just the disguise if you're giving a cylinder-shaped gift to a child — the famous British red pillar-box (mailbox). You could of course adapt the idea and make a rocket, for example. Cut a strip of thin red cardboard to fit around your gift; secure it around the gift with sticky tape. Draw a circle for the lid, larger than the diameter of the cylinder; cut a line to its centre as shown.

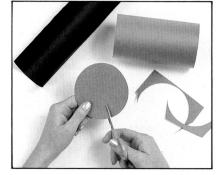

Overlap the cut edges slightly to form a shallow cone, then fix with sticky tape on the wrong side. Wrap one end of the post-box with black paper, folding it over to prevent the present from falling out. Put double-sided tape around the inside of the lid and stick in position. Add a narrow black rectangle for the posting slit and a white rectangle for the notice of collection times.

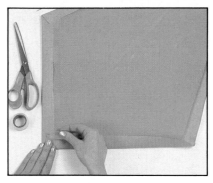

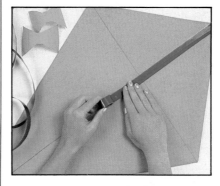

Here's another clever idea for disguising a record. Get two large squares of cardboard; the side of a box will do. Position the record in one corner as shown and draw a line from the bottom right corner of the record to the top right corner of the cardboard. Draw a second rule from the top left corner of the record to complete the kite shape. Repeat for the other square.

Cut out the shapes and sandwich the record between them. Cover one side in coloured paper, folding over the edges and fixing them with sticky tape on the reverse. Cut another piece of paper slightly smaller than the cardboard shape; glue it in position on the back of the kite.

Draw two lines joining the four corners of the kite, and put contrasting tape along them; take care not to stretch the tape as it will pucker the paper. Cut out as many paper bow shapes as you want for the kite's tail. Attach the bows with double-sided tape or glue to a length of ribbon and stick the tail in position behind the longest point of the kite.

A cake, plus candle, is just the right disguise for a birthday present! First, make a drum-shaped frame for the cake; cut a strip of thin cardboard just wider than your present, curl it in a circle big enough to cover your gift and stick it in place with sticky tape. Cut a circle to fit as a lid; attach it with strips of tape.

Cut a strip of white paper to cover the sides of the drum and glue it in position. Tuck one edge of the paper under the open end of the drum and trim the other edge close to the top of the drum to leave a small turning. Cut a series of small nicks in the turning and fold the flaps over, taping them to the lid. Cut a circle slightly smaller than the circumference of the drum and glue it in place.

Place the present inside the cake and put it on a cake stand. Cut two lengths of cord to fit round the circumference of the cake and glue the ends to prevent them from unravelling. Glue one piece to the top of the cake to form 'icing', and the second piece around the bottom, to fix the cake to the stand. Finally, put the candle in the holder and pierce through the centre of the cake.

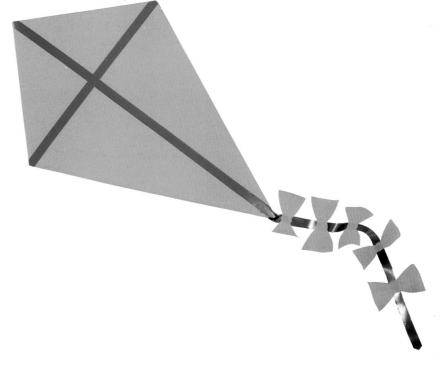

The decorative details on a gift can make all the difference to the finished article. The gift wrap might be bright and jolly, but if the present has no decoration it can look very dull. Even a pretty bow can provide the finishing touch, turning a plain parcel into a chic gift.

Buying ribbon pom-poms can make gift wrapping very expensive. Instead, try making your own decorations. In this section you'll find instructions for different types of decoration, using ribbon, tassels, foil, paper, flowers, and even pot pourri, tights (pantyhose) and sweets! Looking for a special finishing touch for a Christmas or Easter gift? Try the novel designs on pages 110 and 111.

Reels of gift ribbon can be turned into a vast array of different decorations; from stunning rosettes that you couldn't distinguish from shop-bought versions to individual and original pom-poms. Braid, cord, tissues and even candy can be used to decorate your gifts and make parcels that extra bit special.

RIBBON RINGLETS

RIBBON POM-POMS

Apom-pom bow adds a cheerful touch to a present of any shape or size. Use the kind of ribbon which will stick to itself when moistened. Cut seven strips; four measuring about 30cm (12in), the other three about 23cm (9in). You'll also need a small piece of ribbon about 5cm (2in), for the central loop.

Overlap the ends of each of the long strips and moisten them; stick them together to form a loop. Moisten the centre of each loop and stick it together as shown. Cross two of the looped strips, joining them at the central point. Repeat with the other two loops. Join both crosses together so the loops are evenly spaced apart.

Here is an easy way to achieve a very pretty effect. Choose three colours of narrow ribbon which co-ordinate with your gift wrap. Using one ribbon, tie it around your parcel in the usual way, crossing it underneath the parcel and knotting it tightly on top; leave long ends. Tie a length of different coloured ribbon to the centre point, then do the same with a third colour.

Continue tying on lengths of ribbon so that you end up with two lengths, (that is, four ends) of each colour. Tie the central knots tightly to keep them as small as possible. Pull a ribbon length gently along the open blade of a pair of scissors; this will cause it to curl into ringlets. Repeat with each length until they are as curly as you want.

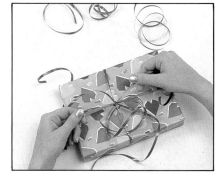

Loop the three shorter lengths, and cross them over each other, fixing them together at the centre. Stick the resulting star in the middle of the large rosette. Fill in the centre with the tiny loop. Obviously, the length and width of ribbon can be varied, according to the size you want the finished pom-pom to be.

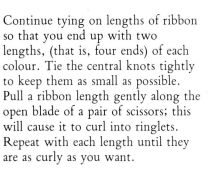

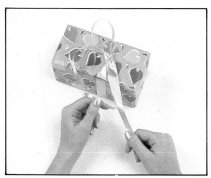

An alternative is to use wide gift ribbon. Tie it round the parcel once, making sure that the knot is as neat as possible and leaving long ends. Cut two small nicks in the ribbon, dividing it evenly into three; pull it to split the ribbon up to the knot. Run each of these lengths along the blade of a pair of scissors until they form ringlets.

TWISTED TRIM

This trimming can be made to match or contrast with the wrapping. You will need the type of ribbon which sticks to itself when dampened; choose whatever colours you like. The smallest strip of ribbon measures about 20cm (8in); cut it out and twist it into the shape of a figure '8'.

Twist the ribbon shape to form a point at each end as shown, then secure it in position by dampening the tape. Cut the next strip, about 7.5cm (3in) bigger; repeat the process. Put the smaller shape on top and in the centre of the new shape; fix it in place.

Make four other figures-of-eight, cutting each one about 7.5cm (3in) longer than the last. Pile them all up and fix them together in the centre. Put the decoration on your gift and attach it by wrapping ribbon round it and the parcel. Finally, arrange it so that each loop is raised above the others and not overlapping as they're inclined to do!

A POINT TO REMEMBER

You couldn't distinguish this pointed pom-pom from a shop-bought version — yet it's a fraction of the price! Use ribbon which sticks to itself when moistened. Make a small loop by wrapping the ribbon round your thumb; moisten the ribbon and fix it in place. Now twist the ribbon back on itself to form a pointed loop, as shown; stick it in position.

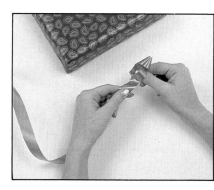

Go on looping the ribbon in twists, spacing them evenly as you go. It is fairly fiddly but keep trying — you'll soon master the technique. You'll probably need to wait a minute between each fixing for the ribbon's glue to dry before turning the next loop.

Continue winding outwards in a circle until the bow is as big as you want; cut off the ribbon, leaving a small tail just visible. Attach the pom-pom to the present with double-sided tape.

ELIZABETHAN BOW

FLOPPY BOW

The scrolled shapes of this decoration are reminiscent of the curlicues embellishing Queen Elizabeth I's signature. Wrap up your present, and choose some gift wrapping ribbon to match or contrast with the colours of the gift wrap. Hold the end of the ribbon in one hand, and form a loop as shown, leaving a small tail.

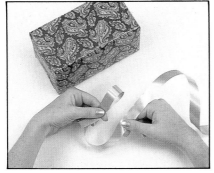

Make a corresponding loop below, forming a figure-of-eight shape. This will be the size of the finished product; adjust the proportion of the loops at this stage if you want a bigger or smaller bow. Continue folding loops of the same size until you have as many as you want — seven at each end is usually enough.

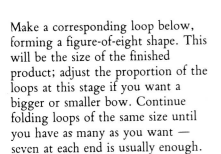

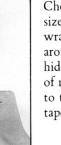

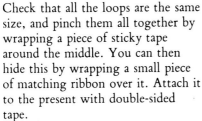

Check that all the loops are the same size, and pinch them all together by wrapping a piece of sticky tape around the middle. You can then hide this by wrapping a small piece of matching ribbon over it. Attach it to the present with double-sided tape.

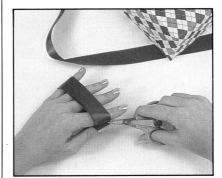

This bow, with its floppy loops, gives a soft, casual effect. You'll need about 2m (6ft) of acetate or craft ribbon, 2.5cm (1in) wide. Cut off about 30cm (12in) ribbon; wind the rest round your fingers. Holding the ribbon firmly, make a notch in both edges with a pair of scissors as shown, cutting through all the layers of ribbon.

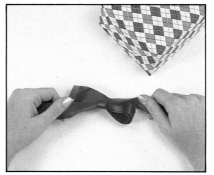

Take the ribbon off your hand and notch the edges of the opposite side of the loops. Flatten the loops so that the notches match in the centre and loops are formed either side. Take the 30cm (12in) length of ribbon and tie it tightly around the notches as shown.

Starting with the innermost loop on one side of the folded bow, gently pull each loop away from the other loops and into the centre of the bow. You'll end up with each loop being visible, thus forming the shape of the finished rosette.

It's hard to believe that these pretty flowers and the butterfly are made from tights (pantyhose) and fuse wire. Cut up a pair of discarded tights or stockings. Cut some 15 amp fuse wire into lengths, some shorter than others, suitable for making petals. Make a circular shape out of each length and twist the ends together.

Put a piece of stocking material over a wire circle and pull it tight, making sure that the whole circle is covered. Fix it in position by firmly winding matching cotton around the twisted stem of the wire. Cut off the excess fabric.

Take seven petals, smaller ones in the centre, and bind them all tightly with thread. Bend the petals around until you're happy with the look of the flower. Tie up your parcel with ribbon and attach the flower with double-sided tape. The butterfly is made in just the same way: two pairs of 'petals' are bound together with thread, then bent into the shape of wings.

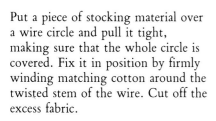

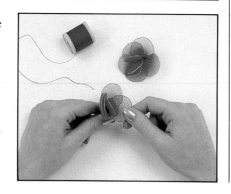

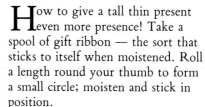

How to give a tall thin present even more presence! Take a spool of gift ribbon — the sort that sticks to itself when moistened. Roll a length round your thumb to form a small circle; moisten and stick in position.

Make another ring, larger than the first; stick that down too. Make another circle, and another, ensuring that their increase in size is in the same proportion each time. Four circles is about the maximum the ribbon can take before flopping slightly and thus losing the crispness of the decoration.

LOOPING THE LOOP

PAINT AND MATCH

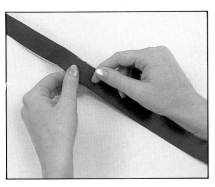

Though this decoration looks best on a rectangular gift. Take 66cm (26in) of woven ribbon; lay it flat. Measure 13cm (5in) from one end of the ribbon and mark both edges. Then mark along the ribbon's length a further 10cm (4in), 7.5cm (3in), 5cm (2in), 7.5cm (3in), 10cm (4in). Using one piece of thread, pick up tiny stitches at each mark along one edge.

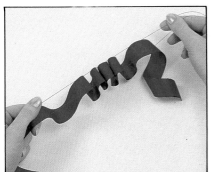

Run a similar gathering thread up the other edge of ribbon, making sure that the stitches are exactly level on both sides. Gather up the loops as shown; it's easiest to knot the two threads together at one end of the gathers and ease the loops along.

Pull the thread tight to make properly-formed loops; sew the joins in place and cut off the excess thread. Tie the ribbon around the gift and use double-sided tape to attach the loops in the centre of the long side of the gift. Snip a diagonal cut at the ends of the ribbon tails.

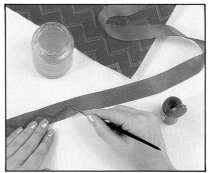

It is quite easy to paint wide ribbon to co-ordinate with your wrapping paper. And the results are stunning! Choose a gift wrap with a simple design. Decide whether you want the ribbon to be a positive version of the paper's design, like the blue example shown here, or a negative one, like the black and white suggestions. Experiment with poster paint on your chosen ribbon.

Keep the design very simple and stylized. When you're happy with your pattern, paint enough ribbon to wrap up the gift, allowing sufficient for a fairly large bow. Leave the ribbon to dry thoroughly before tying it around the parcel. If the paint does crack a little when tying up the ribbon, simply touch it up and leave it to dry again.

CREPE PAPER RUFFLE

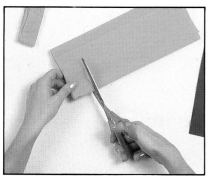

Crepe paper is the ideal material to make a stylish ruffle. There's such a range of colours to choose from, too. For each ruffle, cut two strips of crepe paper, one a little wider than the other. They should both be half as long again as the circumference of the parcel.

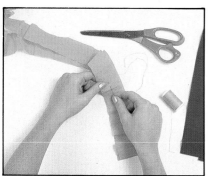

Lay the two strips flat, with the narrower one on top. Sew them both together with matching thread, running a gathering thread down the centre. Gather the strips slightly.

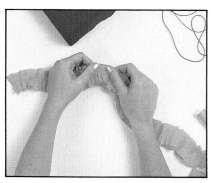

Gently stretch the crepe between both hands along the entire length of the strip; this will create a more ruffled effect. Do each strip separately, then make another ruffle. Wrap the ruffles around the gift, sticking the ends with tape. Tie narrow cord in the middle of the strips to hide the gathering stitches; fluff up the crepe ruffles either side.

RIBBON ROSETTES

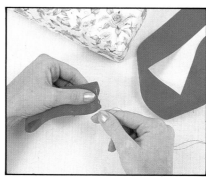 

A winning idea for any gift! Cut a length of fairly wide ribbon; you'll need about 30cm (12in) for each rosette. Fold it in half with the right sides of the ribbon together; sew up the two ends to form a seam.

Using tiny stitches, gather up one edge of the ribbon. Pull the gathering thread tight, arranging the rosette into a neat circle as you do so. Finish it off by sewing across the base. Make as many rosettes as you need and attach them to your parcel with double-sided tape.

A small posy of pretty rosebuds is always acceptable — make as many as you like! Cut a small length of ribbon — about 6-9cm (2-3½in), depending on the width of ribbon you've chosen. Fold the ribbon in half, right sides together, and join the two ends with a small seam. Run a gathering thread around one edge.

Pull the gathering thread tight to form the rosebud; sew it firmly across the base. Make another two or three buds and sew them all together at the base; you may need to add the occasional supporting stitch at the top edges to hold the buds close together.

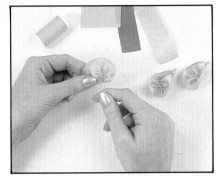

The leaves add an attractive contrast. They are made from a strip of green ribbon, two corners of which have been folded over to form a point. Fix with double-sided tape since glue can leave a mark on ribbon. The illustration below shows the rosebuds grouped on a length of ribbon twice the width of the flowers, set off with narrow green ribbon.

W hat do you do when you haven't any gift wrap and the shops are shut? You use newspaper! The flower on top gives the parcel a stunning and stylish finish. To create the flower cut several lengths of newspaper, some about 15cm (6in) wide, some a little narrower. Fold one strip in half lengthways, and make a series of cuts along its folded edge as shown here.

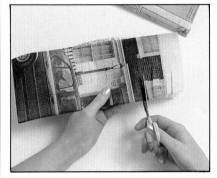

When you've cut along the whole length, roll up the resulting looped fringe. Secure it at the base by winding a piece of sticky tape round it. Fluff out the 'petals' of the flower.

Use up all the strips of paper in the same way. Gather the sections together, smaller ones on the outside. Join them all with tape; leave the ends unstuck and use them to attach the flower to the gift. You can even match the paper to the recipient; use a financial newspaper for a businessman, a comic for a child, a glossy magazine for a lady of leisure.

POINTED STAR

Craft foil is the perfect material for creating this decoration. Use a compass to draw four circles; the ones shown here measure 8cm (3in), 6.5cm (2½in) 5cm (2in) and 4cm (1½in) in diameter. Draw an inner ring of 2cm (¾in) in the centre of each circle. Rule lines to divide the circles evenly into eighths; cut along the lines to the inner circle to make eight segments.

Roll each segment of the circle into a cone; use a dab of glue to secure it. Make sure that each cone shape has a good sharp point by rolling it fairly tightly. The process is a bit fiddly; you may find it easier to roll each cone around the point of a stencil to give it shape. Repeat with the other circles.

Starting with the largest star shape, glue all the stars inside each other, positioning the points of each star between those of the preceding ones. When the glue is dry, gently bend each cone of the middle two stars towards the centre, to fill in the central space, so forming a semi-circular three-dimensional star.

SWEETS FOR MY SWEET

A sweet treat for children of all ages! Boiled sweets (hard candies) with plain cellophane wrappers look best because of their clear colours, but you can use alternatives such as toffees or peppermints. Select five or six of the chosen sweets, and hold them in a bunch by one end of their wrappers.

Take a narrow piece of ribbon and tie all the sweets together tightly; if the wrappers are a little short it may help to bind them first with sewing thread. Leave a reasonably long piece of ribbon on each side of the bunch of sweets so that you can attach it easily to the parcel.

Tie the same ribbon around the parcel, leaving the ends long, then tie the sweets to the centre point as shown. Curl up each ribbon end by pulling it gently along the open blade of a pair of scissors. Try to co-ordinate your gift wrap with the chosen confectionery — black and white paper with humbugs, for example, would look very attractive.

You can make these decorations in a single colour, but they look more effective if you choose several. For each twist, you need three squares of tissue for the outer colour, two for the middle colour and two for the inner (most visible) section. The squares needed for the inner section are smaller than those for the outside; the middle leaves must be of a size in between.

Pick up the squares in order, putting one on top of the other; outer colour first, then the middle, then the inner squares. Position them so that the corners of each square are at a different angle, as shown. Put a couple of stitches through the centre point to secure all the squares together and leave some thread hanging.

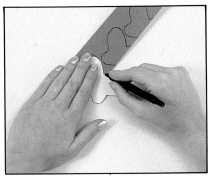

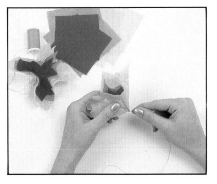

An interesting effect is achieved by attaching three-dimensional decorations all over your parcel. Wrap your gift in plain coloured paper. For the butterflies, take a strip of contrasting plain paper and fold it in half. Draw a butterfly shape on thin cardboard; cut it out and trace round half of it as shown on to the coloured paper. Draw as many as you want to cover the gift.

Cut out the butterfly shapes and fold them on both sides of the half-way fold, to give them bodies. Use glue or thin strips of double-sided tape to attach them in a random pattern to the parcel. Alternatively, tie lots of little bows of the same size using contrasting ribbon; scatter them over your gift using double-sided tape.

Fold the whole thing in half and half again, twisting the folded point at the base to form the shape of the 'flower'. Pull the thread out at the point, and wind it tightly around the twisted base to secure it; 'fluff' out the finished decoration. Make several 'flowers' and group them together on your present.

An added bonus on this gift is the sweet-smelling pouch of pot-pourri. Select some fabric which will tone with your gift wrapping paper. The fabric should be fine, but not loosely woven; the scent of the pot-pourri can then easily diffuse through the material, but the petals and dust can't. Cut out a piece of fabric measuring about 15-20cm (6-8in) square.

A pretty arrangement of dried flowers is a lovely idea for somebody with an autumn or winter birthday. You can pick grasses and seedheads in the country or you can dry flowers from your own garden; it's fun and quite easy. Or you can buy them, though of course it's more expensive that way! Cut the dried plants all the same length.

Put enough pot-pourri in the centre of the fabric to make a generous sachet — a good handful should be just right. If you can, choose a perfume which will match your present — rose pot-pourri would be ideal for a rose bowl, lavender for lavender-scented soaps. You could even use dried herbs to create a bouquet garni for a cookery book!

Bunch the flowers together; when you're happy with them, wrap sticky tape around the stalks. Hide the tape by winding ribbon over it. Tie ribbon round the parcel, finish off with a knot, and attach the little bouquet by tying its trailing ribbons over the knot; trim the ends of the bouquet ribbon away. Using the ends of the other ribbon, finish off by making a pretty bow over the bouquet.

Pick up the four corners of the fabric to form a bundle. Wind sewing thread tightly around the neck of the bundle, and knot the thread securely. Tie the pot-pourri bunch very firmly in case the recipient uses the bag later in her wardrobe. Hide the thread by tying a piece of ribbon around it to match the ribbon on the parcel. Tie the pot-pourri to the gift using a little more matching ribbon.

Paste the recipient's age in a great big number on the side of their present so that *everybody* knows how old they are! Draw around the present, so that you know exactly what size the numbers must be to fill the side of the gift and make a big impact.

Draw the appropriate number using a ruler and measure carefully. Choose thin cardboard or plain paper in a contrasting colour to the wrapping paper.

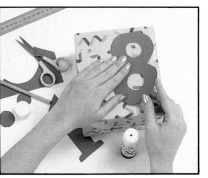

What a lovely bonus to receive with a gift — a beautiful fresh flower. This works most effectively with a long, thin present, showing off a single bloom to perfection. First choose your flower. Trim off any excess leaves and, in the case of roses, thorns. You should end up with just one sprig of leaves.

To prevent the flower from staining the gift wrap or making it damp, wrap the end of the stalk with cling film (plastic wrap). Then cut a narrow strip of matching gift wrap; wrap it around the length of the stalk, fixing it at the back with tape. Cut a small 'V' shape at the top of the paper tube, and attach the bloom to the parcel with double-sided tape.

Cut the numbers out and stick them in position on your gift. You could make a numerical tag to match. This idea could be adapted for use with gifts celebrating wedding anniversaries — 25, 50 and so on.

Holly leaves are an attractive shape and perfect for decorating a festive gift. Measure the length of the diagonal across the top of your parcel. On a sheet of plain paper, draw a large holly leaf, the 'vein' of which measures slightly more than half the length of the diagonal.

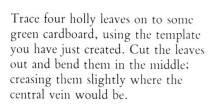

These Christmas bells ring out gaily from your present. Make two paper templates, both bell-shaped, with one showing the outline of the clapper from the bottom edge. From thin cardboard, cut out two of each shape.

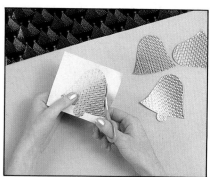

Trace four holly leaves on to some green cardboard, using the template you have just created. Cut the leaves out and bend them in the middle; creasing them slightly where the central vein would be.

Cover all the cardboard shapes with gold paper (or any colour which would co-ordinate with your wrapping paper). Cover both sides, and trim away all the excess paper. On the bell shapes with the clapper, cut a slit from the curved top of the bell to the centre of the bell. On the others (the plain ones) cut a slit from the middle of the bottom edge, also to the centre.

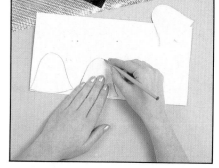

Make the berries from a ball of cotton wool (known as absorbent cotton in the United States) wrapped in two squares of red tissue paper. Put a dab of glue inside and twist up the tissue tightly at the base. When the glue is dry, cut off as much excess of the twist as possible. Group the leaves and berries on the parcel; attach with glue or double-sided tape.

Pierce a hole in the top of the plain bell shapes and thread them with a length of ribbon. Then slot the pairs of bell shapes together (i.e. the plain one, and the one with the clapper) so that they form three-dimensional shapes, as shown here. Tie a group of as many bells as you like on to your gift. This idea can also be used for decorating a wedding gift.

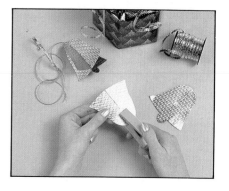

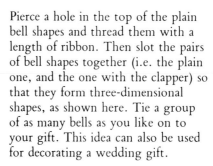

ANGEL'S MESSAGE

SPRING CHICK

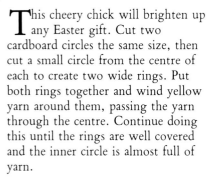

This cheery chick will brighten up any Easter gift. Cut two cardboard circles the same size, then cut a small circle from the centre of each to create two wide rings. Put both rings together and wind yellow yarn around them, passing the yarn through the centre. Continue doing this until the rings are well covered and the inner circle is almost full of yarn.

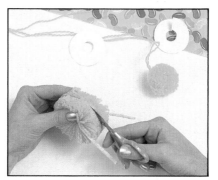

Snip through all the yarn along the outer edge of the cardboard rings. Pass a length of yarn between the two rings, wind it tightly around all the strands of yarn and tie it firmly, leaving long ends. Cut off the cardboard circles and fluff out the ball. Make a bigger ball for the body from two larger rings, and before cutting, pass a pipe cleaner through the rings to form the legs.

Tie the two balls together firmly. Bend the 'legs' up at the ends and wind a section of pipe cleaner around each foot leaving a V-shape on either side so that each foot now has three 'claws'; paint the feet and legs red. Make eyes and a beak out of felt and glue into position. This would work just as well with a Christmas robin decoration, using red and brown yarn.

A heavenly messenger bears the greetings on this Christmas present. Cut a quarter section of a circle from light cardboard to form a narrow cone for the body. On a folded piece of paper draw one arm and one wing against the edge of the fold as shown, so that when they are cut out you will have a pair of each.

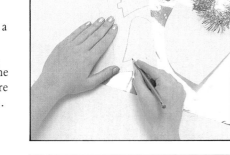

Make the cone and cover it with silver paper (aluminium foil would do). Trace the arm and wings on to silver paper; cut them out and glue them in their relevant positions on the body.

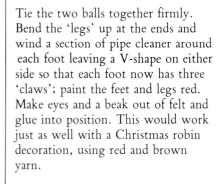

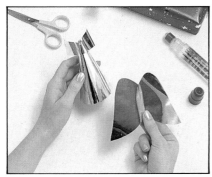

Make the head by rolling up some white tissue paper into a firm ball, twisting the ends of the tissue tightly to form a 'neck'. Glue the head into the top of the cone. Tie a scrap of tinsel into a loose knot and stick it on the head as a halo. Make a scroll from white paper, write on your message and stick it between the angel's hands. Attach the angel to the gift with double-side tape.

It's important that your gift is labelled clearly so that the right present goes to the right person — and that that person knows who the present is from! But there's no need to deface the wrapping paper on your gift by scrawling your message all over it.

Any well-wrapped gift needs a proper tag. It's easy to make one to go with your gift wrap; five methods are suggested in this section. Or perhaps you could tailor-make a tag especially designed for the person receiving the gift. And what a novelty to be able to *eat* the tag afterwards — well, here you will find two kinds of edible tags.

Personal and original gift tags really do make a difference to the finished parcel, as this selection demonstrates. And with a little flair and imagination you can create a wide range of attractive designs.

Give your presents a co-ordinated appearance by creating matching tags. For simple fold-over tags you need to select wrapping paper which has a small design. Take a piece of gift wrap and rule a rectangle on it, twice the width of the required tag. (Outline a section of the design where the motif is visible when isolated.) Ensure the corners are perfect right angles, then cut the tag out.

Paste the tag on to thin cardboard; choose a colour which picks up a shade in the gift wrap. When the glue is dry, cut around the piece of gift wrap. Fold the card in half and punch a hole in the corner. Thread a ribbon through the hole and tie it on to the gift. Alternatively, you can cut out a single image, stick it on to cardboard and cut around the butline, as with the panda tag.

If you have a long message for the recipient of your gift, this fold-out tag allows lots of room. Select a gift wrap design that has a fairly large repeat. One motif must have sufficient space around it so that it can be cut out without including any others. Draw a rectangle around the motif, ensuring that all the corners are right angles.

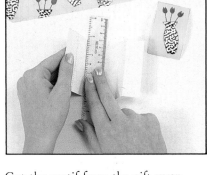

Cut the rectangle out with a craft knife. Next, cut out a piece of thin cardboard the same height as the chosen motif and exactly three times its width. Fold the cardboard in three widthways, creasing the folds well, then fold the top two sections back on themselves, as shown. Mark the folds in pencil first to be sure they are straight.

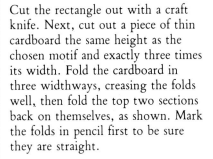

Cut the motif from the gift wrap precisely in half. Glue each half on to the top two sections of the folded card. They should fit exactly, but if necessary trim the top and bottom to form a straight edge. Try matching the colours of the lining cardboard with the gift wrap; in the example shown here, red or even black cardboard could have been used, instead of white, for a different effect.

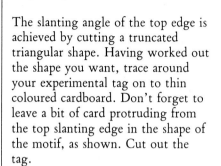

Incorporate a motif from the design of your gift wrap to make a fun three-page tag. It will work with any design involving a trailing string — balloons, kites, balls of yarn and so on. The motif is stuck on the sloping top edge of the middle 'page' of the card. Cut out the motif from gift wrap. Then experiment with a sheet of white paper to get the best shape for your card.

The slanting angle of the top edge is achieved by cutting a truncated triangular shape. Having worked out the shape you want, trace around your experimental tag on to thin coloured cardboard. Don't forget to leave a bit of card protruding from the top slanting edge in the shape of the motif, as shown. Cut out the tag.

Score the two fold lines of the tag using the back of a craft knife and crease them firmly. Glue the motif in position on the middle page and draw a long string trailing down. Close the card and draw another string on the front, making sure it is continuous with the string on page two. Write the recipient's name as if it were part of that string.

There is such a variety of stickers on the market that you're sure to find one which will make an ideal label for your gift. Take a piece of thin coloured cardboard; this will form the background for the sticker. Draw a rectangle on to the cardboard, twice the width you wish the finished tag to be.

Cut out the rectangle with a craft knife and score down the centre to form the fold; crease well. Remove the sticker from its backing and place it in position on the front of the tag. Punch a hole in the back 'page' of the tag, near the fold. Write your message inside and hang the tag on the gift.

There can be no doubt who these presents are for! It's fun to make a tag out of the initial or — even better — the whole name of the recipient. First draw the shape of the letters you want on to a piece of tracing paper. Make sure that the letters in a name interlock sufficiently.

When you're happy with the result, trace the letters (or single initial) on to coloured cardboard, pressing hard to make a clear outline. Use a ruler where there are straight sections to a letter.

Create a stylish effect by matching the tag to the ribbon. Plain ribbon with a strongly patterned paper is attractive but a tartan ribbon with plain paper can look stunning. And if you don't have any ribbon, even a strip of fabric cut out with pinking shears will suffice! Glue a length of ribbon or fabric on to thin cardboard to make it rigid.

Trim away any excess cardboard. Fold the stiffened ribbon over and cut it to the length you want the finished tag to be. Punch a hole through your newly-created tag and thread a piece of contrasting narrow ribbon through the hole to tie it to the parcel. Trim the edges of the tag to match the ends of the bow.

Next, cut out the shape using a craft knife, carefully following the traced lines. Punch a hole in a position where the weight of the tag will make it hang well on the gift.

One way to eat your words — or at least your name! Shortbread is the basis for these edible labels. Sift together 100g (4oz, ½ cup) of caster (fine granulated) sugar and 150g (6oz, 1½ cups) of plain flour into a bowl. Rub in 100g (4oz, ½ cup) of butter till the mixture resembles fine breadcrumbs. Add water to make a stiff dough, knead well and roll it out on a floured board.

Cut out various shapes for the tags, using either pastry cutters or paper templates. Don't forget to make the holes for threading the ribbon later. Bake at 200°C, 400°F or gas mark 6 for 15-20 minutes or until golden brown; leave to cool. Then write the name on, using icing in a piping bag, or simply with a paintbrush dipped in food colouring. This recipe will make 15-20 labels.

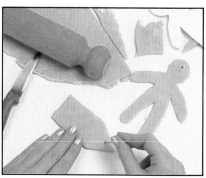

Children will enjoy eating these gift tags made of royal icing. Separate an egg and sift 225g (approximately ½lb, 1¼ cups) of icing (confectioner's) sugar into a bowl. Gradually add a little egg white to make a stiff dough. Knead well, then divide the mixture in two and add food colouring to one half. Knead the icing thoroughly to distribute the colouring.

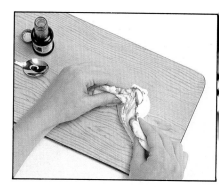

Roll out the icing to about 5mm (¼in). Cut out shapes using small pastry cutters. Colour the other portion of icing if required and repeat. Make a hole in the shapes for a ribbon, then prick out the name with a toothpick or, when the tags have dried, write the name on with a paintbrush dipped in food colouring. Leave the tags to dry out for a week. This makes about 20 tags.

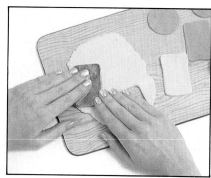

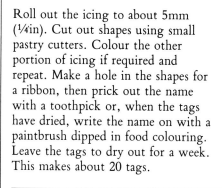

LAZY DAISY

CAMEO

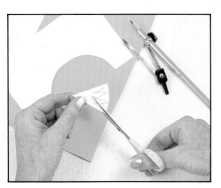

Sometimes the name tag can form the entire decoration for the gift! Wrap your gift in green paper to make a leafy-coloured background for this floral tag. Using a compass, draw a circle that will fit comfortably on top of your present. Fold it in eight and draw four daisy-shaped petals on a segment. With the circle still folded, cut the petals out. This is your template.

Victorian ladies created beautiful pictures using pressed flowers. Why not make a miniature version for a pretty gift tag? Pick up a selection of flowers and leaves and lay them face down on blotting paper. Press another layer of blotting paper on top, keeping the flowers as flat as possible. Place the flowers between the pages of a heavy book and leave them for at least a week.

Draw two circles of the same diameter as the template, and trace the daisy pattern on to them; cut them out. Repeat the process with a smaller circle, to provide two inner layers for the daisy. Pile the daisies on top of each other, arranging them so that none of the petals overlaps, then stick them together in the centre with glue or double-sided tape.

Take out the flowers. Make a template for a perfect oval by folding a small sheet of paper in half and half again; draw a curve across the corner as shown and cut it out. Trace round the unfolded shape on white cardboard, and make a slightly larger oval from coloured cardboard to match the gift wrap.

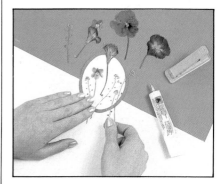

Cut out a circle from yellow paper, write the recipient's name on it and fix it in the centre of the flower. Gently bend up the petals around the yellow centre. You could adapt the idea in mauves to make a Michaelmas daisy, or autumn colours for a chrysanthemum.

Stick the two ovals together, so that the larger one forms a frame for the tag. Arrange the pressed flowers on the white oval to your satisfaction. Glue the flowers in position, using a tube with a very fine nozzle; leave the arrangement to dry thoroughly. Punch a hole in the top of the tag, write the message on the back and tie it to the gift.

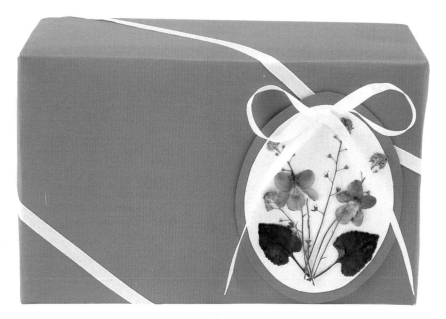

With so many presents being exchanged at this time of the year, tags become even more important. What about some special seasonal ones? Draw any festive shape you like on to thin cardboard; this one is a Christmas stocking. Cut out the shape and cover it with bright paper; try to co-ordinate the colours with those in the gift wrap you use for your present.

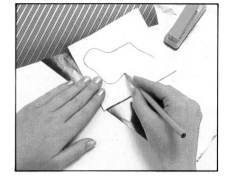

This dotty Christmas cracker can be traced from template 47 and transferred to brightly-coloured card. Cut out, fold down centre and score. Use pinking shears to trim ends of cracker. Cut three strips of florist's ribbon to fit across cracker. Pink edges, spray glue and attach to cracker. Trim excess ribbon.

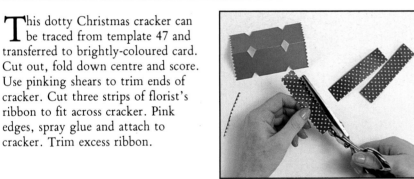

If your wrapping paper has a particular theme in its design make a tag to echo it. To ensure that your design is symmetrical, fold a piece of paper in half and draw on half the design against the fold. Cut around the outline through both layers of paper; open out and use this as a template for the design. Cover a piece of light cardboard with gift wrap and trace around the template.

Tie two pieces of gift-wrap ribbon around 'ends' of cracker, as shown. Split ribbon down centre and curl each length.

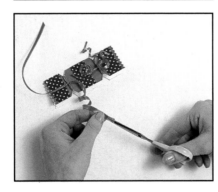

Cut around the outline and punch a hole at the top of the tag. Write your message and tie the tag on to the parcel. You could cheat a little when designing the shape of your tag by tracing an illustration from a magazine or by using the outline of a pastry cutter.

Cut a card 15 by 7.5cm (6 by 3in), score and fold 7.5cm (3in). Cut a piece of sequin waste to fit and attach to card with spray glue. Colour in circles with felt-tipped pens. Many different patterns can be made. Punch a hole in back and thread with ribbon, if desired.

EASTER BUNNY

AHOY THERE!

Knowing who this parcel is for is plain sailing! Fold a strip of thin cardboard in half and draw a stylized boat on to it. Cut it out and stick the ends together with tape, making a three-dimensional boat. Make two creases in the 'bottom' of the boat, along its length, to give it stability.

Cut out a paper sail. For the mast, join two cocktail sticks or toothpicks with tape; break off half of one of them. Stick the mast on to the sail with more tape, leaving the pointed end of the mast at the bottom.

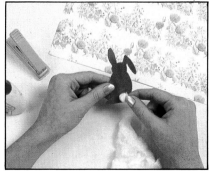

This cute rabbit tag tells the kids who their Easter present is from. Draw the shape of a rabbit on to white cardboard; if you're not good at drawing, you could cheat by tracing the outline of a rabbit from a magazine or book illustration. When you're happy with your design, cut it out.

Either paint the bunny shape, or cover it with brown paper (or whatever colour suits your gift wrap; a red or even green rabbit would be fun). Next take a piece of cotton wool (absorbent cotton) and roll it into a ball for the tail; stick it in position with a dab of glue. Make a hole in the rabbit's head for some ribbon, write your message and tie the tag to the gift.

Add a flying pennant to the top of the mast with paper, and write the recipient's name on the sail. Attach the mast by putting some Plasticine or modelling clay in the bottom of the boat; dig the mast into it. Hide the Plasticine with a small piece of cardboard to match the boat. The finishing touch is the wave made of cotton wool (known as absorbent cotton in the United States).

Personalized cards made with care and affection are always a delight to receive and many of the designs on the following pages are special enough to frame and keep on permanent display.

Over 20 attractive, multi-purpose greeting cards, including invitations and quick cards (pages 136–139), are followed by lots of ideas for cards to celebrate calendar events – Christmas, New Year, Valentine's Day, Easter, Mother's Day, Father's Day and Thanksgiving – and other special occasions, such as birthdays, new home, engagement, new baby, wedding anniversary and retirement. You will find templates for the cards on pages 162–167.

Card comes in a variety of finishes: cloud effect, metallic, parchment style, textured, glossy and matt. The cards on the following pages use tissue, brown, origami, marbled, wall and wrapping paper, as well as foil and cellophane, to create different effects and textures. As an alternative to making your own base cards, card 'blanks', complete with front windows, are readily available from craft shops and good department stores.

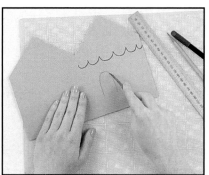

A detachable finger puppet of a jolly circus clown will delight a child. Cut card 18 by 25cm (7 by 10in). Score and fold 12.5cm (5in). Mark 5.5cm (2¼in) down sides of folded card. Measure across the top 6cm (2½in) and mark. Cut through both thicknesses of card to form apex of 'marquee'. Draw roof of marquee with felt-tipped pen. Cut a 'stand' for puppet on front of card.

Trace out templates 7, 8 and 9 and transfer onto thin card to make your own templates. Cut out two balloons from card and satin ribbon strings. Using turquoise felt, cut two hats, two hands and a bow-tie. Cut two heads from white felt; two circles, one for his nose and one for his hat, from pink felt. Cut eyes from narrow black satin ribbon.

Glue balloons and ribbons in place. Sandwich the clown's hands between the two pieces of felt for the head, holding in place with a dab of glue. Sew, with a running stitch, round the clown's head. Glue on hat, bobble, eyes, nose and bow-tie. Place clown on stand and he will appear to be holding the balloons.

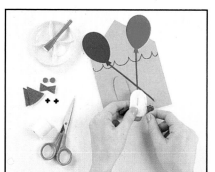

The card is a ready-made 3-fold with window. Cut out circle in left-hand section to match window. Trace out template 43. Put masking tape in each corner to hold tracing still, then place silk over tracing, holding it firm with masking tape. Trace through onto silk using a soft pencil.

Place silk in an embroidery frame and draw over lines of design with gutta. This will stop the silk paints from running into each other. Leave to dry thoroughly — it may take an hour. A hairdryer will speed up the process.

Shake or stir fabric paints and using a clean damp brush flood each petal area with paint in one swift stroke. When paint is dry place a piece of fabric under silk and iron on wrong side for two minutes to set paint. Wash out gutta from silk and dry if you wish. Trim to just larger than window, stick down fabric and left-hand card section with double-sided tape.

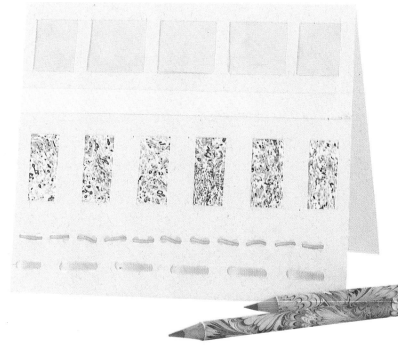

Beautiful paper bags, too pretty to throw away, can be turned into greeting cards. Here, delicately-patterned wallpaper is used to advantage as a background. Cut card 20 by 30cm (8 by 12in). Score 15cm (6in) across and fold. With small scissors carefully cut out your favourite flowers and some leaves.

Cut wallpaper background, leaving small border of card showing. Mark a small dot at each corner with a sharp pencil, so you will easily be able to line up the background.

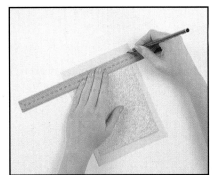

Spray glue on to background wallpaper and stick down on to card using pencil dots as a guide. Spray backs of roses and arrange. If you lay a clean sheet of paper over the card and smooth over the fresly-glued pieces, the edges will not catch on your hands.

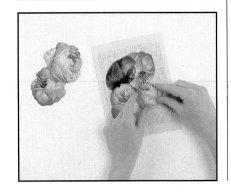

Cut card 15 by 25cm (6 by 10in). Score and fold 12.5cm (5in) across. On inside of card rule four sets of double lines and one single at each end, the depth of weaving strip. Use an even number of slits to start and finish on the inside. Vary depth for second line of slits. Rule two lines, one with 14 dots 9mm (^{3}/sin) apart, second with 10 dots 16mm (^{5}/sin) apart.

Any unusual papers can be used for weaving through the slits, particularly paper you have marbled yourself. Cut paper strips, ribbon and cord slightly longer than width of card, and carefully cut slits and punch holes.

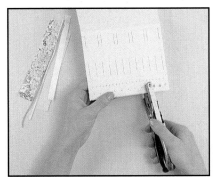

Still working from the inside weave paper, ribbon and cord and finish with a dab of glue. Trim any overhanging ends. On the front of card, glue a strip of ribbon between the two lines of woven paper.

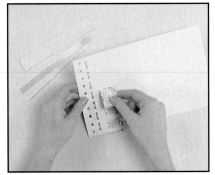

WOVEN SILK

NEEDLEPOINT IN LILAC

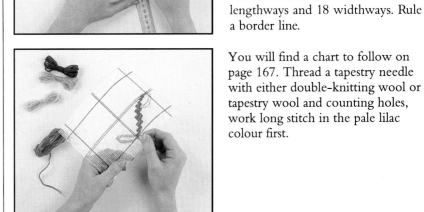

Use mono thread 'lockweave' needlepoint canvas 8 holes to 2cm or 10 holes to 1in, cut 18 by 14cm (7 by 5½in). Find centre of canvas and mark centre hole on four sides. Draw two crosses in different colours either side of centre and side holes. Without counting centre hole, count 29 holes either side lengthways and 18 widthways. Rule a border line.

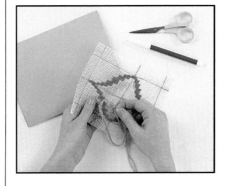

You will find a chart to follow on page 167. Thread a tapestry needle with either double-knitting wool or tapestry wool and counting holes, work long stitch in the pale lilac colour first.

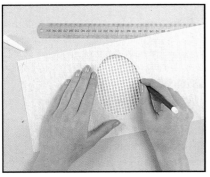

Offcuts of shot silk or other fabrics are woven into a landscape of green fields, hedges, yellow corn, blue sky and pink evening sunset. A ready-cut, 3-fold card was used. Mark top left-hand corner inside card with cross. Cut canvas about 10cm (4in) square. Lay card with oval aperture over canvas and mark edges lightly. Rule a square just outside these marks.

Continue working towards centre, finishing four corners last. Cut a 3-fold card 45 by 20cm (18 by 8in), score and fold at 15cm (6in) intervals. Measure finished piece and cut a slightly smaller window in centre panel of card. Trim canvas to 6mm (¼in) all round and mount using double-sided tape. Close card and stick down.

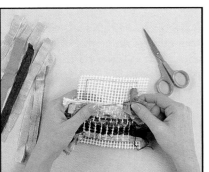

Cut stips of fabric approximately 1cm (½in) wide and 12.5cm (5in) long. Do not worry if they fray as this adds to the charm. Thread large tapestry needle and starting from the bottom weave green strips. Continue with yellow fields, hedges and sky.

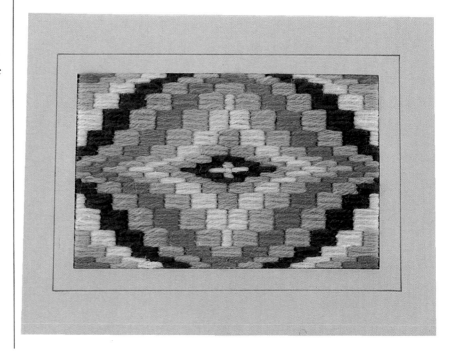

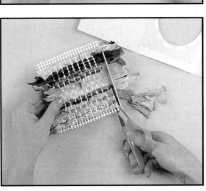

Attach double-sided tape around oval window and along three sides of panel, as shown. Trim canvas 6mm (¼in) outside the ruled square and peel off backing from double-sided tape. Stick canvas in place and close card — the left side with the cross is the side to fold in. Smooth from folded edge to outside so that card stays flat.

Cut card 30 by 13cm (12 by 5in), score and fold 15cm (6in). With fold on top find centre and mark with pencil dot. Measure down 6cm (2½in) on each side. Rule a line from each side point to middle mark to form roof. Stick down ribbon forming a mitre at apex of roof. Cut two pieces of medium weight wrapping paper 20 by 7.5cm (8 by 3in).

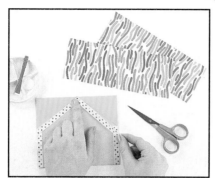

Trace out templates *11* and *12*. Fold length of wrapping paper in half then in half twice more. Draw on half boy or girl making sure hands are on folds. Cut out. When you draw the second child, check folds are in the opposite direction, so that when they are opened they are left and right of card. Open out boys and girls and refold alternate ways.

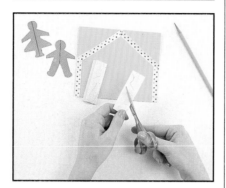

On green and pink paper cut a boy and girl. Glue them to the blank side of the folded figures. Glue the last girl and boy to the card so that their feet are on the bottom edge. Fold figures flat to fit in an envelope.

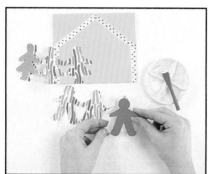

The attraction of this card lies in combining circles cut from a variety of materials of a single colour. The feather adds a final touch of frivolity. Cut card 23 by 18cm (9 by 7in), score and fold 11.5cm (4½in). Find sequins of different sizes but similar colours, then paper, sequin waste, satin paper and foil. Sequin waste can be marked with dividers.

Draw circles of different sizes on your chosen materials. Any round objects can be used for this, or use a pair of compasses. Cut out.

Position circles and sequins to make an interesting arrangement and glue in place. Finally glue on a feather of matching colour.

Cut yellow card 22 by 33cm (8½ by 12¾in). Score and fold 11cm (4¼in) and 22cm (8½in). Trace out template *10*, transfer to thin card to make template. Place over folded card, mark with sharp pencil around balloon outline at top and cut with sharp knife through all three thicknesses. Open out card and trace out balloon shapes onto centre panel and cut out.

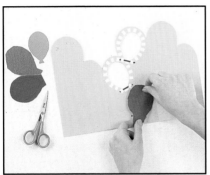

Place double-sided tape in small pieces around the balloon holes on inside centre of card. Cut small pieces of narrow ribbon and stick across neck of balloons. Using balloon template, cut three satin balloons slightly larger. Remove double-sided backing and stick them in place. Stick down left side of the 3-fold card using double-sided tape.

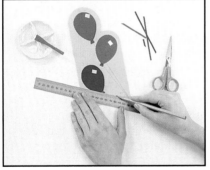

Cut three 'reflection' squares out of white or silver fabric and glue on to the three balloons. Cut four lengths of narrow ribbon, one shorter, so that it will appear to pass behind the red balloon. Using a sharp pencil, rule guide lines for where the ribbons will be placed. Glue them down, leave for a minute or two for glue to dry and then trim ends.

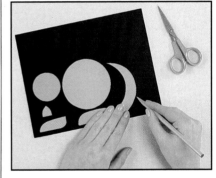

Our mischievous black cat seems not to have noticed the little mouse! Cut card 23 by 18cm (9 by 7in), score 11.5cm (4½in) across and fold along top of card. Trace out cat templates *16-21* and transfer on to thin card to make your own templates. Draw around pieces on to black paper or card. Keep paws and tail the right way round.

Cut out black cat, a tree shape from tissue-paper or card and two green eyes. Mark with a sharp pencil where the pieces will fit on card and stick on in order using spray glue: the tree, body, paws, tail, ears and eyes.

Use stationers' self-adhesive dots for cat's nose and pupils. Finish by drawing whiskers using white chinagraph pencil. Draw around limbs and ears with a soft pencil to make cat stand out.

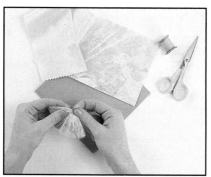

J ust the card to please a young girl who dreams of becoming a ballet dancer. Cut card 30 by 15cm (12 by 6in), score and fold 15cm (6in). Cut skirt from a piece of net 30 by 7.5cm (12 by 3in). Fold in half down its length and press with warm iron. Sew, with small running stitches, along this fold. Make a double stitch to start, gather tightly and finish with a double stitch.

C ut card 22cm (8½in) square, score and fold 11cm (4¼in). Cut out a window 9 by 16.5cm (3½ by 6½in). Trace daffodils from a catalogue or book and transfer onto cartridge paper. Paint with transfer paints. When dry, place over square of polyester or poly-cotton fabric and press with a hot dry iron for two minutes. Carefully lift off paper.

Marbled paper is used for the background. Cut 13cm (5in) square. Cut mirror from silver paper or foil. Details of how to draw a curve are given on page 61. Cut bodice from satin and straps from satin ribbon.

Place print in an embroidery frame the opposite way from hand embroidery and pull until taut. To machine embroider, use same thread on top and bobbin. Take off presser foot and drop 'feed dog' so that teeth will not hold work and you will be able to move it freely. Place embroidery ring under needle and drop pressure leaver.

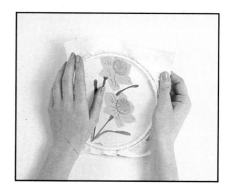

Centre background paper and attach with spray glue. Then glue bodice and mirror. The straps will be easier to put on with rubber-based glue. Mark where skirt is to be attached and pierce two holes each side with dividers. Sew from back of card, tie knot and dab with glue. Make two more holes in the same way for the ballet shoes brooch. Finish with a silver star for a hopeful star.

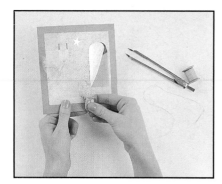

Moving machine wheel by hand, draw up bobbin thread to top and hold to start. Move ring, keeping your fingers on edge of frame and slowly paint with your needle. Experiment with stitches — length 0 and zig-zag are good. Sew outline first then colour in. Press on reverse, mount with double-sided tape and back with white paper.

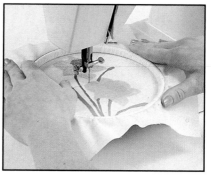

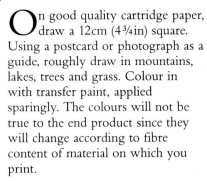

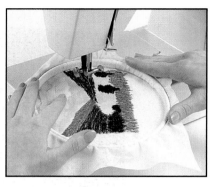

On good quality cartridge paper, draw a 12cm (4¾in) square. Using a postcard or photograph as a guide, roughly draw in mountains, lakes, trees and grass. Colour in with transfer paint, applied sparingly. The colours will not be true to the end product since they will change according to fibre content of material on which you print.

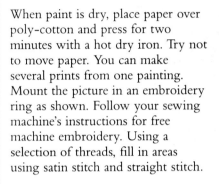

When paint is dry, place paper over poly-cotton and press for two minutes with a hot dry iron. Try not to move paper. You can make several prints from one painting. Mount the picture in an embroidery ring as shown. Follow your sewing machine's instructions for free machine embroidery. Using a selection of threads, fill in areas using satin stitch and straight stitch.

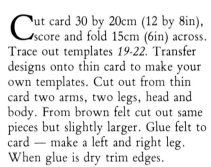

Cut card 30 by 20cm (12 by 8in), score and fold 15cm (6in) across. Trace out templates *19-22*. Transfer designs onto thin card to make your own templates. Cut out from thin card two arms, two legs, head and body. From brown felt cut out same pieces but slightly larger. Glue felt to card — make a left and right leg. When glue is dry trim edges.

Tie ends of satin stitch on back when finished and press. Cut card 14 by 28cm (5½ by 11in). Cut a window 11.5cm (4½) square. Attach finished picture behind window using double-sided tape, then cut a piece of white backing paper and attach to back of your work. Trim excess paper.

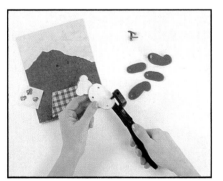

Tear green tissue-paper to resemble hills and hedges and cut gingham tablecloth. Glue them to card and position 'stick-on' flowers. Glue on Teddy's head and punch holes in body, arms and legs. Mark shoulder holes on card, since Teddy will be attached through them. Punch or cut out with a cross, so that brass paper-clips will pass through.

Join Teddy's legs to his body with brass paper-clips. Pass paper-clips through holes at top of Teddy's arms, body and card and open out on back to secure him. Glue on small black beads for eyes and nose. With a fine felt-tipped pen, draw in his snout and mouth.

Diagonal lines of spotted ribbon and self-adhesive labels give this card a 'dotty' air. Cut a piece of black card 25 by 16cm (10 by 6¼in). Score and fold 12.5cm (5in). On inside top left-hand corner measure 4cm (1½in) along top of card and down side edge, mark with dots and score. Fold corner back to outside of card.

Rule a diagonal line across front of card from top left to bottom right. Measure and cut ribbons to fit either side of this line. Cut them slightly longer, to be trimmed later. Cut a triangle of ribbon to fit behind turned-down corner. Spray backs of ribbon with glue in spray booth. Place in position, smooth down and trim edges.

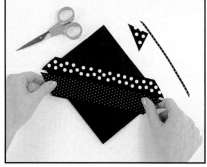

On front bottom left-hand corner of card, stick on self-adhesive dots and also on folded-over, top right-hand corner.

Cut nine heaps of lurex, silk and satin. Cut two pieces of acetate film 10cm (4in) and 9.5cm (3¾in). Draw a 7.5cm (3in) grid of 2.5cm (1in) squares with a chinagraph pencil. Use polyester thread and machine two centre horizontal lines and left-hand vertical. Stuff centre square. Machine right vertical to close centre square. Stuff squares on left; top and bottom centre.

Machine left-hand edge, and then top and bottom edges to close squares. Stuff three right-hand squares and machine right-hand edge to close. Pull threads to back and knot. Trim and put a dot of glue on each knot to hold it.

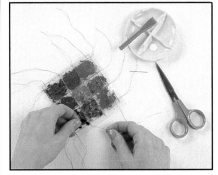

Make or buy a 3-fold card and cut a double window mount. Mark inside top left-hand corner with cross. Put double-sided tape around centre window of card and edges. Pull off backing of tape and place patchwork parcels in window. Close card and add cord and tassel.

PUFFINS

Colourful puffins, cut from a sheet of wrapping paper, keep a lookout from their perch. Cut card 28 by 13cm (18 by 5¼in). The card is blue on the inside and white on the outside. On the outside, from the left, score 9cm (3½in) and 19cm (7½in) across and fold. Turn card over and on the inside, from the left, score and fold 20cm (8in) across.

Cut out three puffins and spray glue the first on outside of far right-hand panel of card, facing right. Cut round him with a craft knife leaving him attached by his tail. The score line on the outside will allow him to stand forward.

Glue the other two puffins in place on the inside. Any wrapping paper with a distinct animal motif can be used in this way to make a striking card.

MATISSE INSPIRED

Cut card 22 by 22cm (8½ by 8½in), score and fold 11cm (4¼in) across. Centre your compass point horizontally 5.5cm (2in) from top of card. Draw an arc so that it touches the sides and top edge of card, then cut through both thicknesses. You could make a template of this shape if you wanted to make several cards.

Brightly coloured origami paper is perfect for this exuberant card. Either draw on back of paper or cut freehand a collection of shapes and colours.

Arrange paper shapes in order of gluing and stick them onto card. Tweezers will help you to apply glue to the tiny star shapes, not your fingers!

Atheme card to give to a musical friend. The treble clefs are buttons. Cut red glossy card 22 by 15cm (8½ by 6in). Score and fold 11cm (4¼in). Draw a square 5.5 by 7.5cm (2¼ by 3in) on white paper. Rule two staves — groups of five lines 3mm (⅛in) apart — using a fine black felt-tipped pen. Cut out the square.

Centre the square of music paper on card so that you have an equal margin on three sides. Visually, it is better to have a larger margin at base of card. Mark corners of music lightly on card and stick down using spray glue. Place opened card on a piece of felt and pierce two holes for the two buttons using dividers or a thick needle.

From the back sew on buttons through the holes you have pierced, then knot the thread and trim. Finish knots with a dab of glue.

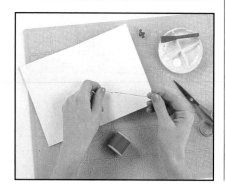

Windows open to reveal flowers cut from wrapping paper which could also wrap a gift. Cut glossy green card 22 by 15cm (8½ by 6in). Score and fold 11cm (4¼in). Cut a 4cm (1½in) equilateral triangle template. Open card flat and on the inside front draw four triangles. With steel ruler and craft knife cut two sides of triangles and score third.

Cut a piece of white paper the same size as the closed card and lay it under the card front. Open up windows and draw the triangles through the windows. These will be your guides for sticking on the pieces of flowered paper. Mark top left-hand corner of inside of card and paper with a cross. Cut out four triangles of flowers.

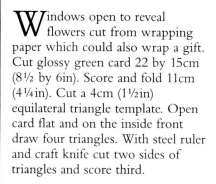

Glue flower triangles on paper where marked in pencil. Place a line of glue along all four edges on front of paper and attach face down on inside front of card. Open up the windows and you will see peeping flowers.

Cut blue card 23 by 16.5cm (9 by 6½in). Score and fold 11.5cm (4½in). Trace templates *2* and *3* for sail and windsurfer. Rub soft pencil over back of tracing of windsurfer, draw over outline again onto grey tissue-paper to transfer image and cut out. Make a template of the sail and draw round onto a piece of mid-blue card.

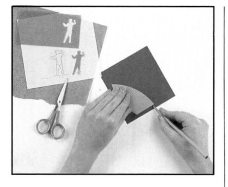

Kites flying in a high spring sky are always a cheerful sight and these three are made from wrapping paper and narrow satin ribbon. Cut pale blue card 22 by 15cm (8½ by 6in). Score and fold 11cm (4¼in). Cut out kites in three different sizes and papers using a ruler. Arrange and stick on card using spray glue.

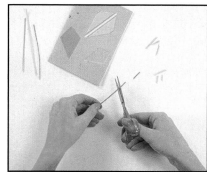

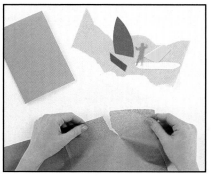

Draw and cut a surf-board from a piece of white card 10 by 1cm (4 by ½in) and curve ends. Cut out sail, and two coloured strips of card to fit diagonally over sail. Tear waves from two pieces of blue tissue-paper — one deep blue, the other a lighter blue. Glue coloured strips on to sail.

Cut narrow satin ribbons slightly longer than card so they will hang below bottom of card. Cut short lengths of ribbon for bows.

Arrange pieces on the main card and mark where they fit with sharp pencil dots. Place all components in spray booth right-side down and spray backs with glue. Place on card in order: dark waves then surf-board, sail, man and pale waves. Place a piece of clean paper over card and smooth pieces flat with your hand. Trim off any excess with craft knife.

Glue and hold in place for a moment since satin ribbon tends to resist glue at first. Some of the bows can be a 'V' of twisted ribbon.

QUILTED LILIES

THANKS WITH FLOWERS

This small piece of quilting is from a ready-printed panel. It will shrink a little when it has been quilted, so measure and cut window from card *after* you have finished the piece. You will need very thin wadding (batting) to back the cotton panel. Cut a piece of card 45 by 15cm (18 by 6in) and score two folds 15cm (6in) apart. Pin panel to a slightly larger square of wadding.

On a larger piece of work, muslin would be used as a backing fabric, but in this instance it has been left out so that there is less bulk inside the card. Working from the centre, tack (baste) the two layers together, making sure the picture covers the wadding.

Cotton thread gives best results in hand quilting. Starting from the centre, with a knot on the back, sew with tiny running stitches. Finish thread with a double back stitch. Take out tacking stitches. Do not press or you will lose quilted effect. Measure finished piece and cut window from centre of 3-fold card. With double-sided tape, stick down quilted panel and back flap of card.

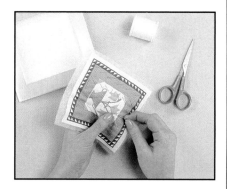

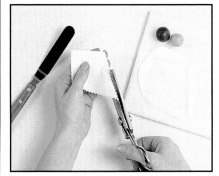

Cut card 22 by 15cm (8½ by 6in), score and fold 11cm (4¼in). Draw border around card, first in pencil then pink felt-tipped pen. Roll out a piece of white Fimo modelling material until thin and cut a kite shape. Cut edges again with pinking shears.

Roll out lots of tiny pink balls for flowers and some long green sausages to be cut for stems. Roll out some flat lengths of pink clay to make bow.

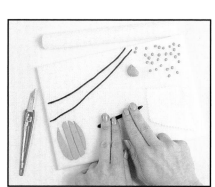

Fashion wrapping paper shape from 'kite' and place on piece of baking foil. Slip green stems inside and press on flower balls with cocktail stick. Make bow by folding pink lengths and shaping. Lay on foil and bake for 15-20 minutes on 130°C (275°F/Gas mark 1) to harden (check manufacturer's instructions). Leave to cool, glue to card and attach bow.

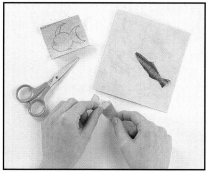

Cut out card 25 by 14cm (10 by 5½in). Score and fold 12.5cm (5in) across. Trace out fish (*4, 5* and *6*) on to the smooth side of bonding web. Cut out fish just outside pencil outline and place rough side of web on to back of your fabric. Press with a warm iron to melt the glue. Cut out on outline. Peel off backing and position on card. Press with a dry iron.

A window-box full of spring flowers is sure to bring cheer. We have used a ready-cut, 3-fold card with window. Fold under left-hand side of card (looking from the inside), marked with a cross in our second picture. With a sharp pencil, draw through window outline and cut out second window using a craft knife and steel ruler.

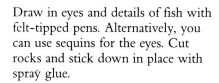

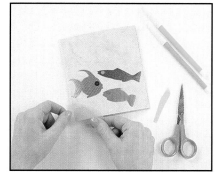

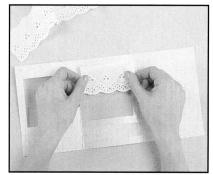

Draw in eyes and details of fish with felt-tipped pens. Alternatively, you can use sequins for the eyes. Cut rocks and stick down in place with spray glue.

Place 1cm (½in) of double-sided sticky tape around centre window and edges of card. Cut piece of broiderie anglaise or lace to fit half the window and a piece of tracing paper cut slightly larger than aperture. Peel off tape backing and stick down curtain, then tracing paper. Peel off tape backing on edges of card and close left-hand side over. Light will filter through.

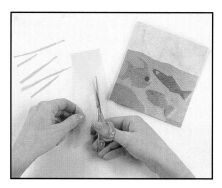

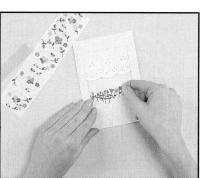

Cut sea and sand from organza and put on to card with spray glue. Trim edges with a craft knife and use offcuts to make sea ripples and waves. **Note**: Be sure to use card of at least 240gsm (160lb/sq in) or the heat of the iron will distort it.

Apply 'stick-on' flowers (purchased on a strip) in a line half on the card and half on the tracing paper, then finish with a strip of satin ribbon or paper for the window box. Add a couple more flowers to the top of the window if you wish.

The mask is double, so that a couple could wear one each, perhaps decorating the plain one themselves. Trace out template *46* and cut a piece of black card 43 by 10cm (17 by 4in), score and fold 21.5cm (8½in). Transfer mask design onto black card and cut out with sharp craft knife through both thicknesses. Mark punch holes.

Cut pink glossy card 15 by 22cm (6 by 8½in), score and fold 11cm (4¼in). Draw out cake shape onto thin card and cut out to make template. Warm a ball of Fimo modelling material in your hands and roll out until thin. Place template on clay and cut round with a knife. Make a little dent in top centre where candle will fix.

Collect together sequins, beads and feathers. Stick them in place with rubber-based glue. Each mask could be different. If you have bought a bag of 'sweepings' you will have a variety of sequin shapes to use. You could also add silver or gold pen designs, scraps of foil, glitter, ribbon cut into shapes — have fun!

Carefully transfer to baking foil with a spatula or knife. Bake cake according to manufacturer's instructions. Cake may stretch, but you can trim with scissors after baking. Glue doiley tablecloth on card. Cut spotted ribbon and fold around base of cake. Attach with double-sided tape or glue and add second ribbon trim.

Punch holes at either side and thread ribbon through front mask. The ribbon should be long and curled by running over scissor blades. It can be re-curled if it flattens in the post. Write your invitation message in gold or silver pen to show up on black card.

Wipe back of cake with lighter fuel to remove any grease. Dab rubber-based glue on back of cake and wait until tacky before fixing to card. Spread a fine line of glue along candle and apply to card. Hold in place for a minute or two until glue dries.

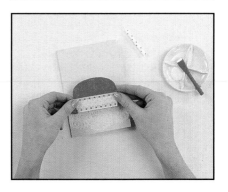

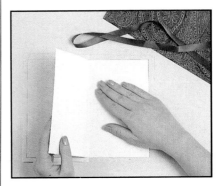

Capture the hosts of the party on a roll of film to make personal invitation cards, each one a little different. The children were delighted to be involved, especially when they opened the 'presents', even though these were empty boxes! Set up props before children come into room. Work fast before they lose concentration. A few small sweets help keep them going.

Make a mask to fit the 'sunken plate' area of the card mount and mark corners of photographs with a compass or sharp pencil point. Cut photograph with a sharp craft knife and ruler and use spray glue to affix.

Beautiful wrapping paper lasts a little longer made into a quick and effective card. Cut card, score and fold. Cut wrapping paper a little larger. Glue wrong side of wrapping paper and lay it flat. Position first half of card on paper and smooth. Bring up wrapping paper to adhere to other half of card but leave room for fold. Smooth down.

Trim edges with a sharp knife. Affix ribbon on four sides on inside of card with a little piece of double-sided tape. Tie ribbon in a bow.

Invitations can be hand-made by children too — a great way to keep them happy and involved in party planning. This rabbit is for an Easter football party given by a nine year-old boy. He drew the picture, then photocopied it a number of times. Each invitation can be hand-coloured before being glued to cards.

Photographs of flowers can be mounted on cards and sent to friends during winter months. Make a collection over the summer. Make a mask of the right size so that you may frame the most effective image. Mark four corners with a compass or sharp pencil point. Cut off excess with ruler and craft knife. Spray glue to mount.

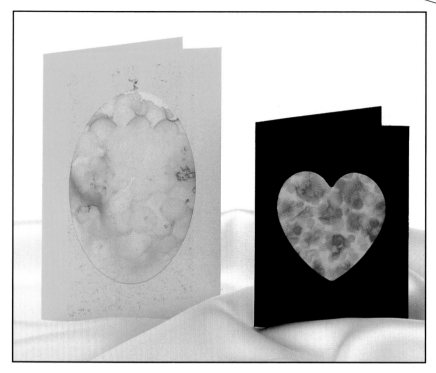

W onderful abstract patterns can be produced by sprinkling salt on freshly painted silk. Cut a piece of fine white silk lining and place in an embroidery frame, pulling taut. Select colours of silk paints you wish to use, shake and carefully open jars. Wet brush in water jar. Apply paint fairly swiftly and immediately sprinkle on salt. Fill frame with designs.

Leave to dry, then brush off salt. The silk will yield a variety of effects, so place different ready-cut window cards over the most attractive patterns. Mark area to be framed in window, then cut out slightly larger. The smaller the window, the more designs you can make. You could also add embroidery, beads and sequins to designs.

Mount silk in centre window of 3-fold card, using double-sided tape. Stick down left-hand portion of card over back of silk.

This magical, ever-rolling landscape is all in the imagination. It is made from layers of torn tissue-paper and plastic iridescent film. Cut pieces of card 16 by 25cm (6¼ by 10in). Score and fold 12.5cm (5in). Roughly tear several strips of tissue-paper and cut iridescent film.

Arrange them on a sheet of A4 (21 by 30cm/8 by 12in) typing paper so that colours overlap and shade. When you are happy with your arrangement, turn strips over and spray glue. You will find one side of tissue-paper has more shine than the other. If there are gaps, you could fill them in with silver pen.

Divide sheet of paper into six or more pieces and cut with a sharp craft knife. Each landscape can now be positioned on a card and glued.

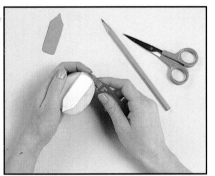

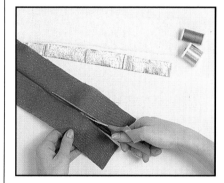

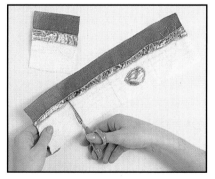

Potato cuts make quick but 'impressionistic' prints. Choose a medium-sized potato to fit comfortably into your hand. Cut in half and lay on it a motif cut from a piece of paper. Cut along edge of image, then slice potato away all round shape so that image is raised. Dry on a paper towel.

A water-based, poster or even fabric paint can be used. Apply paint to potato image, turn over and press gently but firmly onto card. Clean off paint with tissue when you want to change colour and continue, making sure overlapping colours are dry.

Some cards will be better than others, but this is part of their charm. Finish off candle card with gold pen flame and 'surround'. We have also made some cards using eraser lips and hearts — appropriate for a Valentine party.

To make these quick cards even speedier to achieve, we used ready-cut 3-folds, and stickers and buttons to decorate. Cut three strips of fabric in suitable colours: here, blue glitter-spotted material for sky, silver lamé for frozen landscape and white towelling for snow.

Machine the strips together with a wide satin stitch. Machine over twice if you want a thicker line. Measure size of aperture of ready-cut 3-fold cards and mark cutting lines on fabric. Machine trees with lines of stitch, or cut circles of lamé and make ponds. Let your imagination dream up a different idea for each card.

Cut up sections and sew buttons in place or attach stickers. Using double-sided tape, mount pieces and close cards. Extra sequins can be added to borders for moon or stars.

Cut silver card 30 by 15cm (12 by 6in), score and fold 15cm (6in). Trace templates *23* and *24* and transfer onto thin card. Cut 13cm (5in) square of green satin paper and 10cm (4in) square of dark green tissue-paper. Fold these two squares in half twice, then diagonally across to make a triangle.

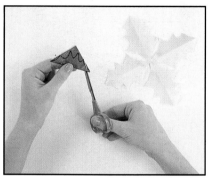

Cut out larger holly from satin paper and unfold, then dark green holly. Hold holly templates in place on paper triangles with paper clips when cutting out. You can draw round the templates first if you find it easier.

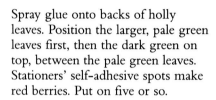

Spray glue onto backs of holly leaves. Position the larger, pale green leaves first, then the dark green on top, between the pale green leaves. Stationers' self-adhesive spots make red berries. Put on five or so.

The snowman at the window invites us to come outside to play in the snow. Cut off left-hand side of this 3-fold card so that light will shine through window. Cut a piece of film slightly smaller than folded card. Draw snowman and trees on to paper to fit between window bars. Place paper under film and on right side draw outline of snowman and trees with silver pen.

Turn over film and colour in trees and snowman using a white chinagraph pencil.

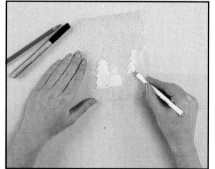

Turn back film onto right side and draw in scarf and nose with a red chinagraph pencil. Add face details in silver. Attach film to inside of card with double-sided tape and place a silver star where it can be seen shining through window.

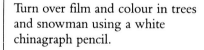

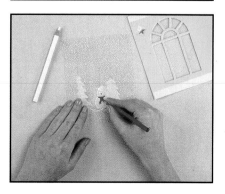

Cut glossy red card 18 by 23cm (7 by 9in), score and fold 11.5cm (4½in) across. Cut on bias four strips of Christmas fabrics 2.5 by 30cm (1 by 12in) long. Fold strips lengthways, machine 3mm (¹/sin) seam allowance. Leave length of thread at end, thread with bodkin and knot. Thread bodkin back through tube with damp fingers.

Cut card 23 by 18cm (9 by 7in), score 11.5cm (4½in) and fold along top. Trace out template *41* and transfer onto thin card to make template. Place on polystyrene wallpaper and draw round with a soft pencil. Cut out with craft knife. Cut out ice caps and ground from iridescent plastic or silver paper.

Thread length of double wool through each tube. Pin ends of tubes to a firm surface. Plait by laying four strands over left hand, take left strand over two middle strands and right strand over one. Continue to end. Ease into a circle, cross over ends and sew through to secure. Trim and finish with a bow.

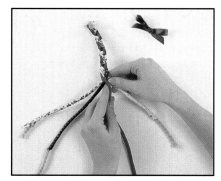

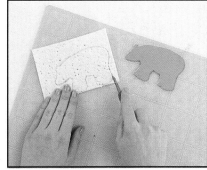

Glue down mountains, ground and polar bear, placing the latter in front of peaks. Glue on silver sequin stars.

Bind trimmed ends with embroidery cotton, tie a knot and trim. Draw an arched border (see page 61) using a gold pen. Centre finished wreath and pierce through card with a thick needle or point of dividers. Sew through from back of card, knot thread, trim and finish with dot of glue to hold firm.

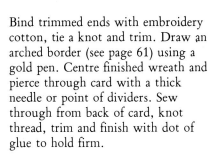

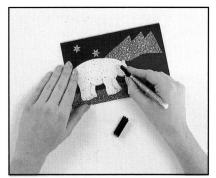

With a silver pen, draw in polar bear's features: legs, paws and ears. The polar bear could also be made from white felt.

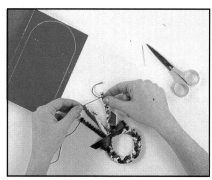

Cut card 18 by 23cm (7 by 9in). Score and fold 11.5cm (4½in). Draw border in silver pen around card. Trace off template 26 and transfer onto thin card. Draw round template onto red felt using a water-soluble pen. It is not easy to mark sequin waste so hold template in place and cut round it.

Cut card 15 by 22cm (6 by 8½in), score and fold 11cm (4¼in) along top. Mark centre top of the card with pencil dot. Cut triangle from sequin waste, place on card and mark two sides at bottom of tree. Glue along edges of tree and hold in place on card until glue dries. Any residue glue can be rubbed away when it is dry.

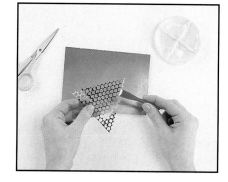

Sew sequin waste to felt by hand or machine, then trim both layers neatly.

Cut a base for the tree from a piece of card or paper. Curl over scissors a number of narrow pieces of ribbon cut about 9.5cm (3¾in) long.

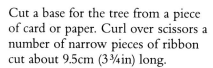

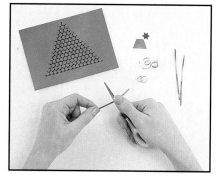

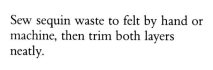

Glue stocking to card, then add the little pony eraser or another small gift that can be glued on. Draw holly and berries using felt-tipped pens. You could also add beads and sequins if you wish.

Glue on base and add sequin star to top of tree. Slip curled ribbons through every other hole in sequin waste and every other row, starting at top of tree. No need to tie them; they will stay in place. You will need to deliver this card by hand or use a box.

On red fabric draw in pencil four 9cm (3½in) squares and cut out. Fold in 6mm (¼in) seam allowance and press. Find centre of square by folding diagonally each way and mark with tip of iron. Fold down one corner to this mark and pin. Continue with other corners to make a square. Catch centre points with a small stitch. Fold in again and sew. Complete all four squares.

This card could be used for the New Year or Christmas. You will see from template 28 that only two sides of the 3-sided card are shown. The left-hand portion is a repeat of the right but with 7cm (2¾in) added to the bottom, so it stands taller. Trace out template adding extra section to make left-hand part of card. Rub soft pencil over back of tracing.

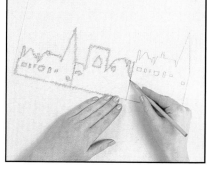

Cut four 2cm (¾in) squares from fir-tree fabric. Place two red squares right sides together and sew down one side to make a double square. Pin fir-tree patch diagonally over seam on right side and curl back folded edges surrounding patch. Slip stitch to hold in place. Repeat to make another double square.

Cut a piece of white card 33 by 15cm (13 by 6in), lay tracing over right side up, lining up lower edges, hold in place with masking tape and draw over outline to transfer drawing.

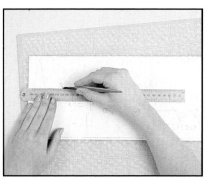

Sew double squares together and place third and fourth fir-tree patches over seams. Sew tiny beads in corners of 'windows'. Cut card 25 by 18cm (10 by 7in), score and fold 12.5cm (5in). Mark top centre and sides 6cm (2½in) down with pencil. Cut through card to form a point. Glue finished square centred horizontally onto card. Add gold border.

Use a ruler to help keep lines straight and cut out. Score and fold into sections. Trim lower edge and 1mm (¹/₁₆ in) from one side of card so that it will fold flat. You will need an extra piece of card in the envelope to protect the points.

Cut card 15 by 20cm (6 by 8in) and score down centre. Trace template *33*, transfer onto thin card and draw round on green card. Cut out using craft knife. Set your sewing machine to a fairly wide satin stitch. Sew moving card from side to side to form garlands. Pull threads through to back, tie off with knot and finish with dab of glue.

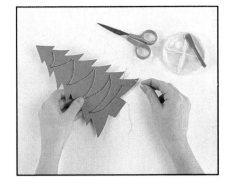

Stick on self-adhesive spots to resemble Christmas tree balls. Cut narrow satin ribbon into 14 1cm (½in) pieces.

A simple, easily-made card in unusual colours for Christmas. Cut card 11 by 20cm (4¼ by 8in), score and fold 10cm (4in). The fold is at the top of card. Cut a strip of green plastic from an old shopping bag. Tear four strips of tissue in shades of orange and yellow. The fir-tree is from a strip of self-adhesive 'stickers'.

Glue them in place at end of branches on back of card. Tweezers will help you to hold them steady. Leave until glue dries. Cut tops diagonally to look like candles. Add the finishing touch — a red star on top of tree.

Arrange strips so that colours overlap and produce new colours and tones. Stick down tree. Spray glue onto back of strips and stick down.

Trim excess paper from edges of card with a steel ruler and sharp craft knife.

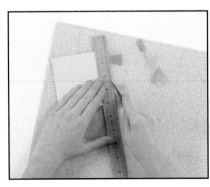

Cut gold card 30 by 15cm (12 by 6in) and score twice 7.5cm (3in) in from each side. Trace out template *25* and carefully work out where the points will fall. Mark design on back of gold card and cut out using a sharp craft knife and ruler for straight edges.

Burnish edges of gold card with the back of your thumbnail if they have lifted. Cut kings' clothes from three pieces of brocade, slightly larger than apertures. Place small pieces of double-sided tape around kings on inside of card and stick brocade in place.

Cut kings' gifts from gold card and glue in place. Attach sequins to points of their crowns. Stick on white card to cover back of centre panel. To protect the points, slip a further piece of card into the envelope. The three kings which have been cut out could be used for a further card, gift tag, or stencil.

New Year celebrations are particularly associated with Scotland. So here, in traditional Scottish style, we have tartan and golden bells for our New Year greeting. A ready-cut window card was used. Remove left-hand section of 3-fold card with a sharp craft knife and ruler. Use this spare card to make two bells.

Cut a piece of tartan fabric or paper to fit inside back of card, attach with spray glue and trim edges. Trace template *27* and transfer on to spare gold card. Cut out and back with tartan using spray glue. Trim with small scissors. Punch holes in bells.

Make a bow from narrow satin ribbon and cut a length for the bells to hang from. Thread first bell and hold in place with a dab of glue. Thread second bell. Sew through bow and ends of the bell's ribbon to hold in place, glue at top of circular window, so that bells hang free.

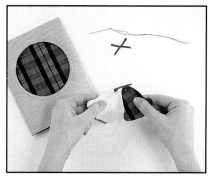

NEW YEAR DOVE

SWEET-HEART

A dove of peace for New Year. It is made from a paper doiley with calendar dates falling from its beak. Cut deep blue card 30 by 20cm (12 by 8in), score 15cm (6in) and fold. Draw freehand two curves at top of card to represent clouds and cut with craft knife.

Trace dove template *42* and transfer to thin card to make your own template. Trace out dove onto white paper doiley and cut out, together with dates 1 and 31 from an old calendar. Add a strip of transluscent film waved along upper edge to resemble hills.

Spray glue all pieces and place on card together with four star sequins. Using a silver pen, draw line along edge of cloud curves.

We used a mould from a cake decorating shop and filled it with tiny cake sweets. Cut a 3-fold card 42 by 19cm (16½ by 7½in), score and fold 14cm (5½in). Tape heart to back of tracing paper. Turn over and rub along edge of heart with soft pencil to make template. Line up heart tracing in centre of middle section of card and transfer outline. Cut out with craft knife.

Place double-sided tape round heart aperture and around edges of left-hand portion of card, marked with a cross. Remove backing from tape around heart and place mould in position. Press to stick firmly. Put narrow line of double sided-tape around edge of heart.

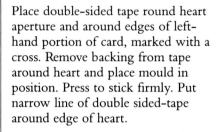

Pour sweets into heart until full and pack out with a piece of wadding (batting) cut to heart shape. Take off backing from tape around heart and from left-hand portion of card, fold over card and press down. A pretty pink bow is the finishing touch.

Cut card 22 by 15cm (8½ by 6in) score and fold 11cm (4¼in). Trace out heart *38* and transfer to a thin piece of card to make your own template. Cut out a heart in thin white card. Place template on front of card at a slight angle and draw round in pencil. Cut round pencil line leaving enough uncut at bottom to enable card to stand.

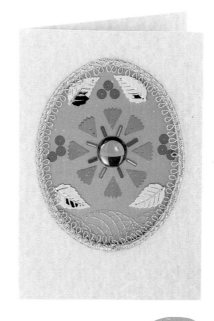

Glue dried flower petals on to white heart working in rows from outside to centre. Use a rubber-based glue; tweezers will help to hold petals steady. Finish with a whole flower in centre.

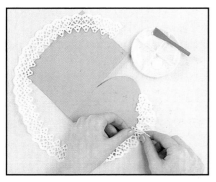

Cut border from a paper doiley. Spread a thin line of glue on outside of main card heart. Pleat doiley border onto glue all round heart. Stick petal heart over pleated doiley, cover with a piece of clean paper and smooth down. Hold for a minute until glue dries. Lastly stick on Victorian angel motif on top right-hand corner of card.

Use a ready-made 3-fold card with oval, egg-shaped window. Place double-sided tape around oval window and edges of inside of card. Peel off backing and attach strip of gold lace to bottom of oval. Cut piece of sumptuous satin slightly larger than aperture, and stick down so that the satin side will show through window.

Glue large, jewel-like bead in centre of 'egg'. Arrange beads, sequin leaves and petals, then glue in position. Tweezers will make it easier to place them accurately.

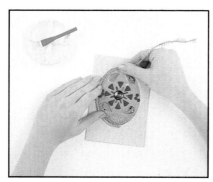

Finish with smear of rubber-based glue around edge of egg on outside of card. Leave for a moment to become tacky, then press down gold braid. Neatly trim end of braid.

A doll's straw bonnet forms the basis of this card and is decorated with spring-coloured ribbons, flowers and a butterfly. Cut card 15 by 22cm (6 by 8½in), score and fold 11cm (4¼in). Cut length of yellow ribbon and cut inverted 'V' shape at ends. Hold in place around hat and sew leaving tails at centre back. Repeat with a length of slightly narrower ribbon.

Trim stems of small fabric flowers and pin in place on ribbon at regular intervals around hat.

A lace sachet of pot pourri could be detached and used later to perfume a drawer. Pot pourri can be bought in a variety of colours and perfumes. Cut card 23 by 18cm (9 by 7in), score and fold 11.5cm (4½in). Cut out two lace flowers, pin together and oversew leaving a gap to fill with pot pourri.

Make a funnel from a piece of paper and fill lace sachet with pot pourri. Oversew to close. Make a bow from narrow satin ribbon and curl ends over scissors.

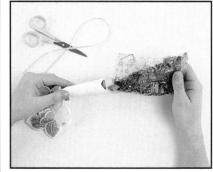

Sew flowers in place using double thread. Finish with butterfly at front. Centre bonnet on card and attach by sewing through brim of hat and knotting threads on inside of card. A dab of glue will make knots secure. Arrange ribbons prettily.

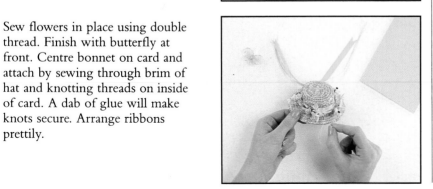

Cut three tissue paper leaves and glue onto card. Sew bow on to sachet. Using a point of dividers or a thick sharp needle, make two holes at either side of card, for positioning sachet. Sew through and knot on back, securing with a dab of glue.

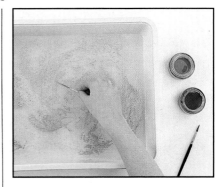

Cut card 22 by 19cm (8½ by 7½in), score and fold 11cm (4¼in) for top. Into a plastic tray put two pints of cold water, mixed with 14g (½oz) of wallpaper paste. Leave for 15 minutes. In a small jar mix 2.5cm (1in) of oil paint from a tube and a little turpentine substitute. Apply drops of the mixed paint onto the surface of the water. Disperse with an orange stick.

Place piece of paper larger than card gently on top of water and remove again fairly quickly, as soon as the paint has taken to surface of paper. Leave to dry on a sheet of newspaper. Press flat, if necessary, when dry. Cut to fit card and glue down.

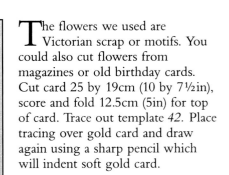

The flowers we used are Victorian scrap or motifs. You could also cut flowers from magazines or old birthday cards. Cut card 25 by 19cm (10 by 7½in), score and fold 12.5cm (5in) for top of card. Trace out template *42*. Place tracing over gold card and draw again using a sharp pencil which will indent soft gold card.

Trace out car from a magazine or postcard and transfer to glossy white paper. Cut out and glue down. Trace 'chrome' details on to silver paper or card, cut out and glue in place. Add details with silver pen.

Measure a border around edges of card and mark in pencil. Go over border again in gold pen.

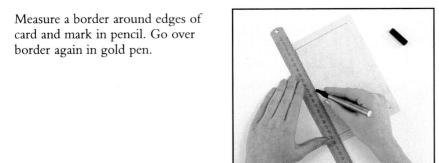

Glue the cornucopia onto the card, then the flowers and fruit tumbling out. Add a white dove.

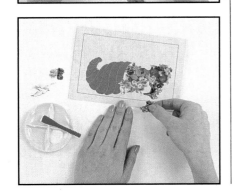

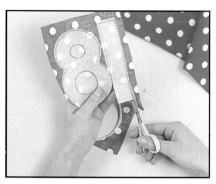

Trace out template *90* onto paper side of bonding web. Cut out just outside pencil outline. Iron onto wrong side of red polka dot fabric and cut out on pencil outline.

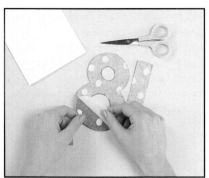

Peel off paper backing to reveal web of glue. Cut a piece of white card 14 by 24cm (5½ by 9½in). Score and fold 12cm (4¾in). Dry iron '18' onto front of card, making sure the '1' is on fold of card. The glue will melt with the heat of the iron. As long as card is not too light, ie, at least 240 gsm (160lb/sq in), the card will not curl.

Open out card and cut round edge of '18' leaving a tiny piece of card to hold together '1' and '8'. When drawing or cutting curves, it is always easier to work towards the body following curve of your hand.

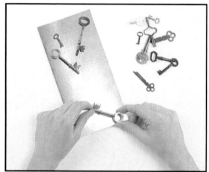

An unusual way to mark a 21st birthday and the traditional receipt of the key of the door. Cut a piece of bright silver card 22 by 22cm (8½ by 8½in) and score fold down the centre. Collect together some interesting shaped keys. Place folded silver card inside and lay keys on card in a pleasing arrangement.

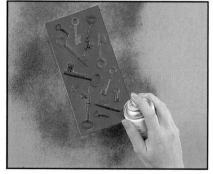

Use spray car paint, holding the can 20-25cm (8-10in) away from card, and spray in a few short bursts to cover the whole card. Allow the first coat to dry for a few minutes and then spray a second coat. To ensure even distribution you should carefully turn the card between coats. You may wish to spray a third coat. Use in a well-ventilated room.

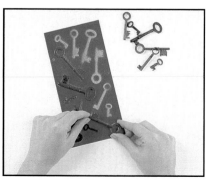

When completely dry, remove keys. You will not be able to get the cellulose paint off the keys easily, so be sure to use keys you no longer need. Other objects, such as old clock and watch parts, can also be used to make theme cards.

Cut grey marble-effect card 28 by 19cm (11 by 7½in), score and fold 14cm (5½in). Trace out template *30*. Cut piece of silver card to fit, turn over and hold down with masking tape. Place tracing over card and attach with masking tape. Trace through onto card with a sharp pencil. Trace base onto a piece of black card.

With a sharp craft knife, cut out cup and base. Burnish edges of silver card by rubbing gently with the back of your thumbnail.

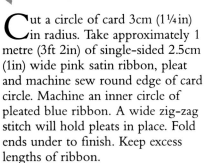

Cut a circle of card 3cm (1¼in) in radius. Take approximately 1 metre (3ft 2in) of single-sided 2.5cm (1in) wide pink satin ribbon, pleat and machine sew round edge of card circle. Machine an inner circle of pleated blue ribbon. A wide zig-zag stitch will hold pleats in place. Fold ends under to finish. Keep excess lengths of ribbon.

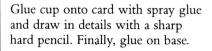

Glue cup onto card with spray glue and draw in details with a sharp hard pencil. Finally, glue on base.

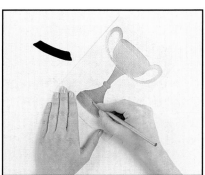

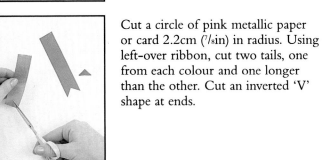

Cut a circle of pink metallic paper or card 2.2cm (⅞in) in radius. Using left-over ribbon, cut two tails, one from each colour and one longer than the other. Cut an inverted 'V' shape at ends.

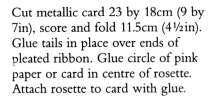

Cut metallic card 23 by 18cm (9 by 7in), score and fold 11.5cm (4½in). Glue tails in place over ends of pleated ribbon. Glue circle of pink paper or card in centre of rosette. Attach rosette to card with glue.

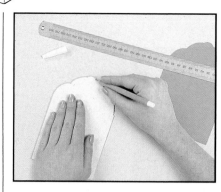

Cut card 22 by 16cm (8½ by 6¼in), score and fold 11cm (4¼in). Trace out template *34* and transfer to thin card adding 10cm (4in) to depth, to match card. Cut out and place on folded card. Draw round church window shape at top of card and cut through both thicknesses. Draw border with felt-tipped pen using ruler for straight edges.

Place several layers of different shades of pink tissue-paper together in a pile on a cutting board. Cut round template *35* to make approximately 10 hearts.

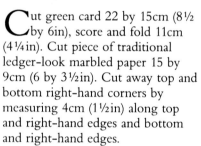

Cut green card 22 by 15cm (8½ by 6in), score and fold 11cm (4¼in). Cut piece of traditional ledger-look marbled paper 15 by 9cm (6 by 3½in). Cut away top and bottom right-hand corners by measuring 4cm (1½in) along top and right-hand edges and bottom and right-hand edges.

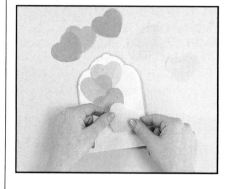

Spray glue hearts and position on card so that they overlap. You could stick more hearts inside card and also leave some loose so that they scatter when card is opened.

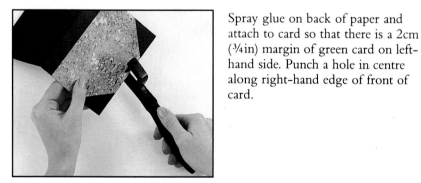

Spray glue on back of paper and attach to card so that there is a 2cm (¾in) margin of green card on left-hand side. Punch a hole in centre along right-hand edge of front of card.

Thread a length of brown satin ribbon through hole and tie into a bow.

Make your own template from our dove *(37)* and cut an extra template for wing alone (see finished card). Draw round dove twice on dark blue felt so that birds face opposite directions and cut out. Cut two pieces of muslin 18 by 11.5cm (7 by 4½in), position doves between two layers and pin. Tack layers together to hold doves in place.

Colours can be matched to those of the bridesmaid's dresses. Cut card 15 by 30cm (6 by 12in), score and fold 15cm (6in). Bind turquoise felt-tipped pen to compass and draw a double circle on centre of card. Sew a line of running stitches along edge of strip of lace half a metre (1ft 6in) in length. Gather into a circle and sew seam.

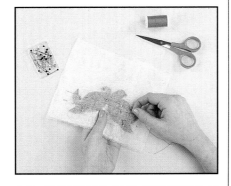

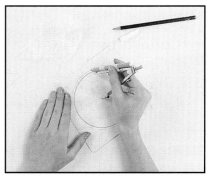

Using two strands of embroidery thread, sew tiny running stitches around doves and stitch feet (see finished card). Place wing template over doves and lightly draw round with a sharp pencil. Quilt along these lines. When finished, take out tacking thread and lightly press.

Sew ribbon flowers onto centre of lace circle. Cut a strip of flower braid into single flowers and sew around ribbon flowers.

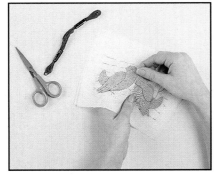

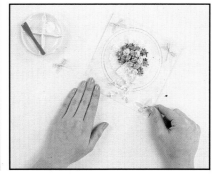

Purchase a 3-fold window card to fit quilted doves. Cut out matching window from left-hand section of card (see page 65). Trim muslin to about 6mm (¼in) larger than window. Check and mark top of window to avoid mounting work upside-down. Stick down using double-sided tape. Add tiny round beads for doves' eyes and pearl beads to corners of window.

Sew on a couple of strings of ribbon flowers or braid to hang from bouquet. Using a sharp needle or compass point, make several holes in card and sew on lace bouquet from back of card using double thread. Tie a knot and add a dab of glue to secure. Glue on satin bows in four corners.

Cut card 45cm by 20cm (18in by 8in). Score and fold at 15cm (6in) and 30cm (12in) to form a 3-fold card. Follow chart on page 167. You may vary the wools and use up odds and ends. Most wool is used double on 12 holes to 2.5cm (1in) canvas. Find centre point of canvas and draw on fireplace design with felt-tipped pens.

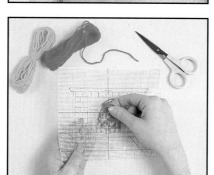

Start in centre, working the fire in random long stitch and tent stitch, varying the colours of the flames. Next, work the fire basket in tent stitch.

Continue with copper fireguard in slanting satin stitch, fire surround in tent stitch, brickwork in long stitch, carpet in tent stitch and walls in long stitch. For the rug, lay a cocktail stick across canvas and work stitches over stick. Cut loops to make pile. When finished, trim and cut a window in 3-fold card to fit piece. Mount with double-sided tape.

Trace out template 36 and transfer outer balloon onto blue card, inner balloon onto white card and also onto tracing paper side of bonding web. Number each segment and cut out. Mark on blue balloon where inner balloon will fit. Iron balloon segments onto wrong side of three fabrics. Cut out carefully and peel off backing.

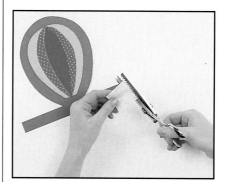

Place balloon segments onto white card balloon and press with a dry iron. Trim edges and using guide on main blue balloon, glue down. Cut a small piece of fabric for basket with pinking shears and glue in place.

Draw in ropes then basket design on fabric using a brown felt-tipped pen. Score base of balloon where indicated on right side and fold back so that the balloon will stand. If being mailed, this card should have an extra piece of card in the envelope for protection.

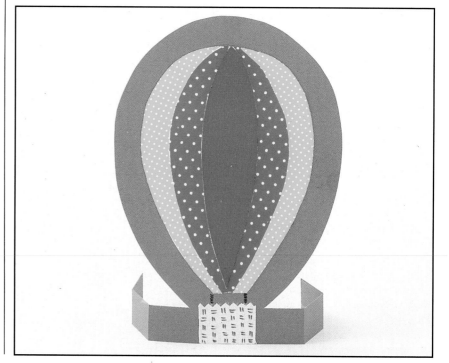

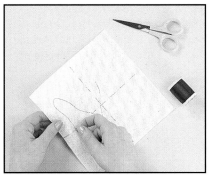

This card is worked in cross-stitch over hardanger fabric, 22 holes to 2.5cm (1in). Use six colours of stranded cotton, two strands thick. Mark centre of fabric by folding in half and running a tacking stitch along fold in both directions through holes. You will find a chart to work from on page 167.

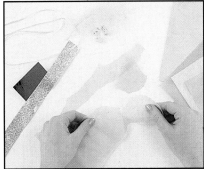

Cut card 23 by 18cm (9 by 7in), score and fold 11.5cm (4½in). This is a spontaneous arrangement, so no two cards will look the same. Lay out a selection of blue materials: ribbon, sequin waste, buttons, feathers, tissue and silver paper. Tear tissue-paper and cut chosen papers into random shapes. When you overlay strips of tissue, more shades of blue will occur.

It is best to work one quadrant at a time, starting at the centre where guidelines cross. Work bottom diagonals of cross-stitch first, then return in opposite direction to form cross. This helps to get an even stitch since the thread tends to wear thin. Do not start with a knot but sew over ends on back as you work. Finish in same way.

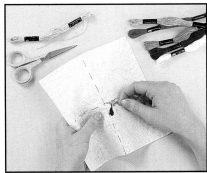

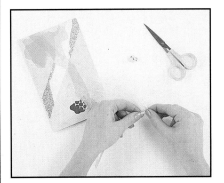

Spray glue your materials and place in your favourite arrangement and trim any excess. Tie a bow from narrow satin ribbon onto base of feather and trim ends diagonally. Attach to card by sewing through.

When complete, remove guideline stitches. Press back of work using a pressing cloth and trim. Cut card to frame oval template *40,* score and fold in half. Cut oval window in front. Mount work with double-sided tape and back with a piece of white paper to fit. Attach with double-sided tape.

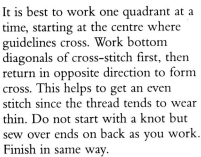

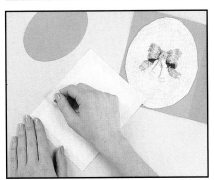

To attach duck button, make two holes with sharp needle or point of dividers, checking which way the button shank lies. Sew on duck button from back using double thread. Finish with a knot and secure with a dab of glue.

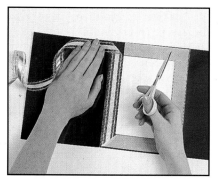

Cut a piece of blue foil card 45 by 20cm (18 by 8in). Score at 15cm (6in) and 30cm (12in) across and fold on outside. Cut out centre window 10 by 15cm (4 by 6in). On outside place double-sided tape around window. Stick down silver ribbon. Mitre corners by folding back ribbon at right-angles and cutting diagonally. Cut next piece of ribbon at same diagonal to fit.

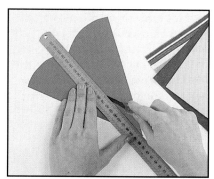

Idyllic leisure-filled days, beachcombing in yellow sand under blue sky. Trace template *39* and transfer to blue card. Score down centre.

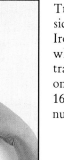

Trace templates *44* and *45* onto paper side of bonding web, then cut out. Iron rough side onto silver lamé and when cool cut out carefully. Peel off tracing paper, turn over and iron onto a piece of silk or satin 11 by 16.5cm (4½ by 6½in), placing numbers so that they overlap.

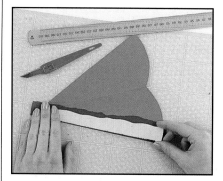

Tear blue tissue-paper to resemble sea. Cut a piece of yellow paper with a curved top edge to make it appear that waves are breaking. Place pieces wrong side up in a spray booth and spray glue. Fix to card and trim to fit.

Set machine to satin stitch and test on spare piece of fabric. Use silver thread on top and polyester thread on bobbin. Use an appliqué or buttonhole foot if you have one. If fabric puckers, place a piece of paper under fabric. When finished knot threads at back. Mount, using double-sided tape and close card.

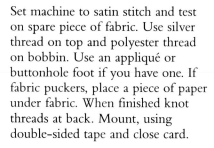

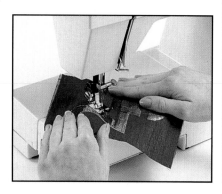

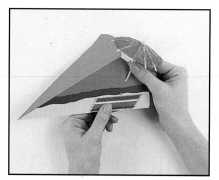

Cut a piece of striped fabric or paper to make a beachtowel. Draw fringe on towel with a felt-tipped pen. Glue in place. Punch two holes and insert beach umbrella.

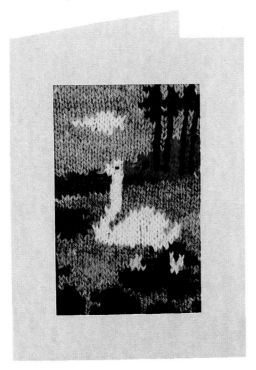

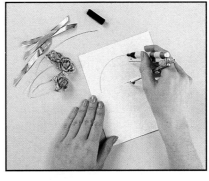

A bunch of golden roses to celebrate 50 golden years together. Cut card 16.5 by 25cm (6½ by 10in), score and fold 12.5cm (5in). Find horizontal centre of card and draw a circle with gold pen taped to compass. Cut three 10cm (4in) pieces of gold gift-wrap ribbon and cut ends diagonally to use as leaves.

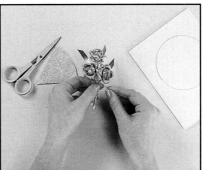

Arrange gold roses with leaves and hold in place by binding together with fine wire. Cut a piece of gold paper in a triangle shape, curving the top.

Cast on 36 stitches and knit in stocking stitch using 4-ply wools, following chart on page 167. Weave different-coloured yarns at back by laying new yarn just under-right-hand needle and looping wool for next stitch around it without making an extra stitch.

Wrap paper around flowers and glue at back to secure. You may like to put a dab of glue to hold roses in place. Apply glue to back of bunch of flowers and stick in place on card. Add golden birds and hearts and a large '50' cake decoration.

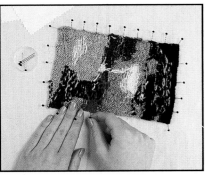

When piece is finished, block it out before pressing on wrong side into a soft surface. Pin all round edges without stretching piece. Press using a damp cloth or steam iron. Leave to settle.

Sew in beak, using yellow wool, and his eye using black wool. Cut card 45 by 20cm (18 by 8in). Score and fold at 15cm (6in) and 30cm (12in) to form 3-fold card. Measure and then cut a window in centre portion. Use double-side tape to attach knitting and close card. Make sure you mount swan the right way up.

The following templates and charts are for the various boxes described in *Boxes, Bags and Envelopes,* one heart-shaped gift wrapping from *Disguises,* and many of the designs from the *Greeting Cards* section. Trace outline onto tracing, greaseproof or layout paper using a sharp pencil, then reverse the paper and draw over the outline again to transfer image onto template card or paper.

Box templates are identified by design name and page number. Draw them carefully, following either the metric or jthe imperial measurements and score along the fold marks (indicated by dotted lines) on the inside of the box with the back of a craft knife or the blunt edge of a pair of scissors. Scale measurements up or down to alter the size of the box. Card templates are identified by a template number only and are given actual size for ease of use. Bold dashed lines usually indicate that only half the template is shown. Charts for four needlepoint card designs are given on page 167.

Diamonds Are Forever (page 89)

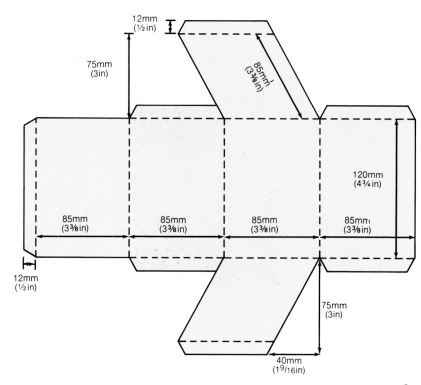

Squared Up (page 88)

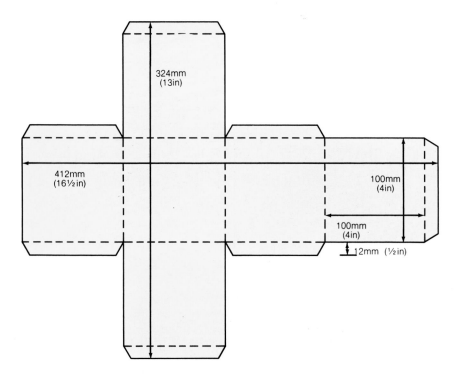

Floral Tribute (page 90)

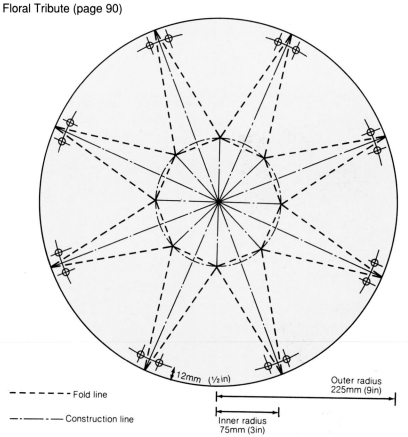

- - - - - Fold line

— · — · — Construction line

Inner radius 75mm (3in)

Outer radius 225mm (9in)

Box Clever (page 88)

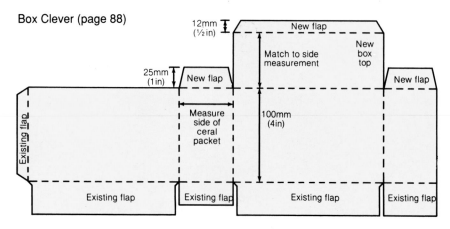

BOX TEMPLATES

Handle with Care (page 90)

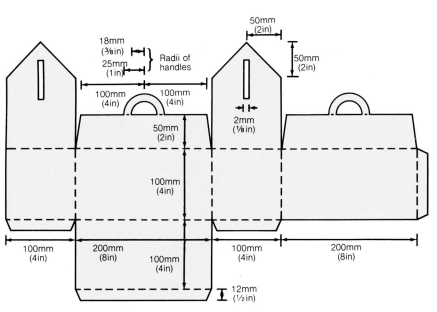

Smart Sachets (page 91)

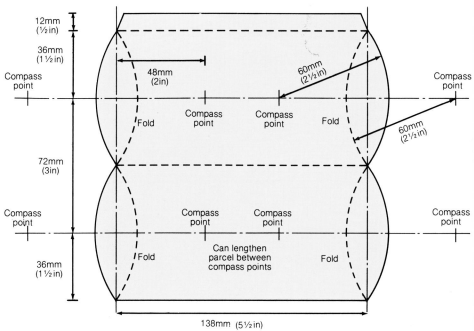

The Pyramids (page 92)

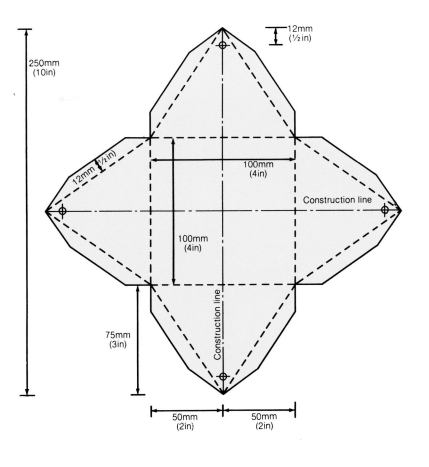

Boxed In (page 93)

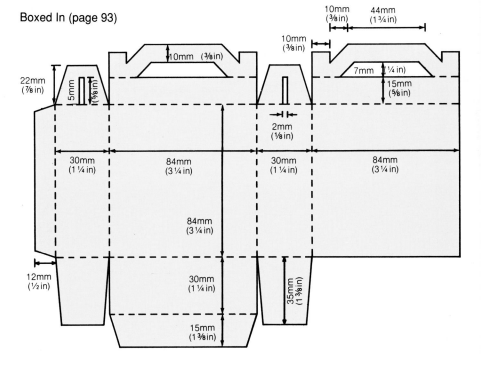

Woven Hearts (page 98)

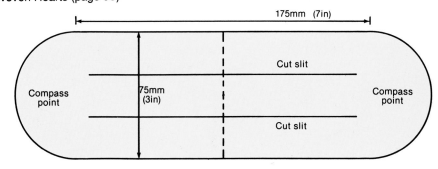

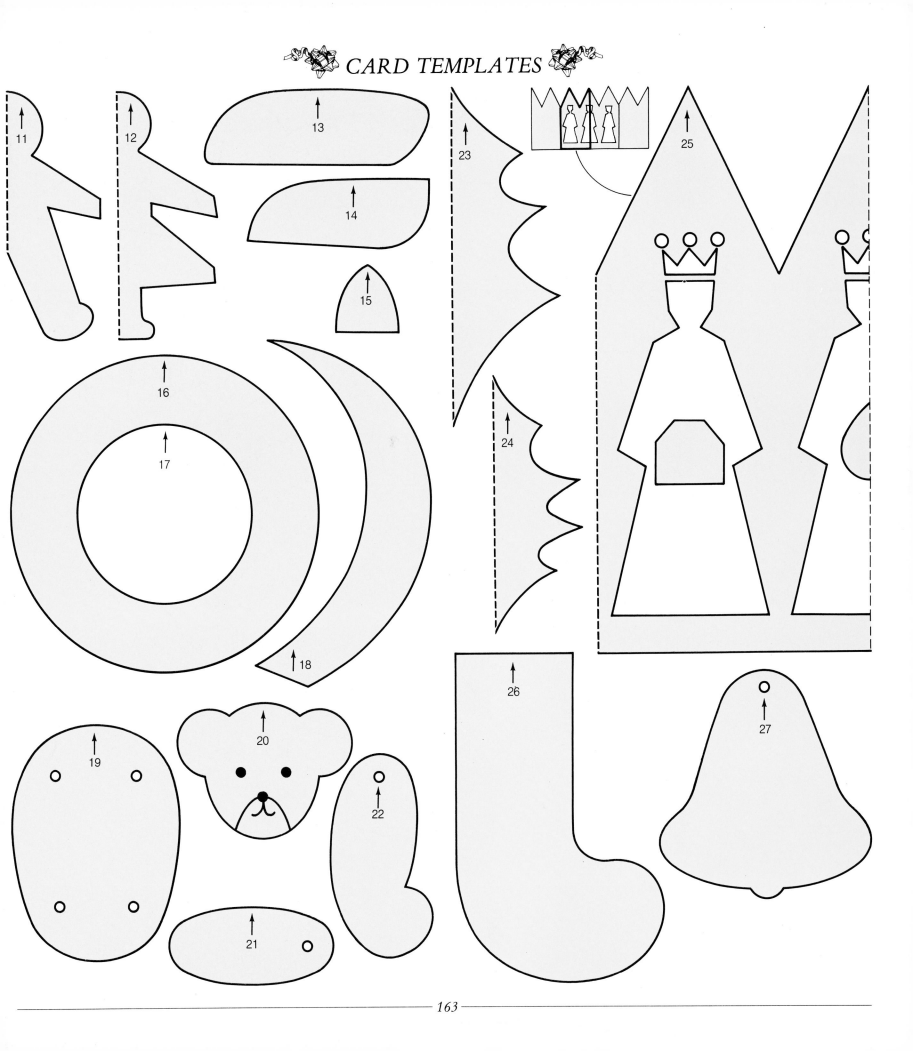

CARD TEMPLATES

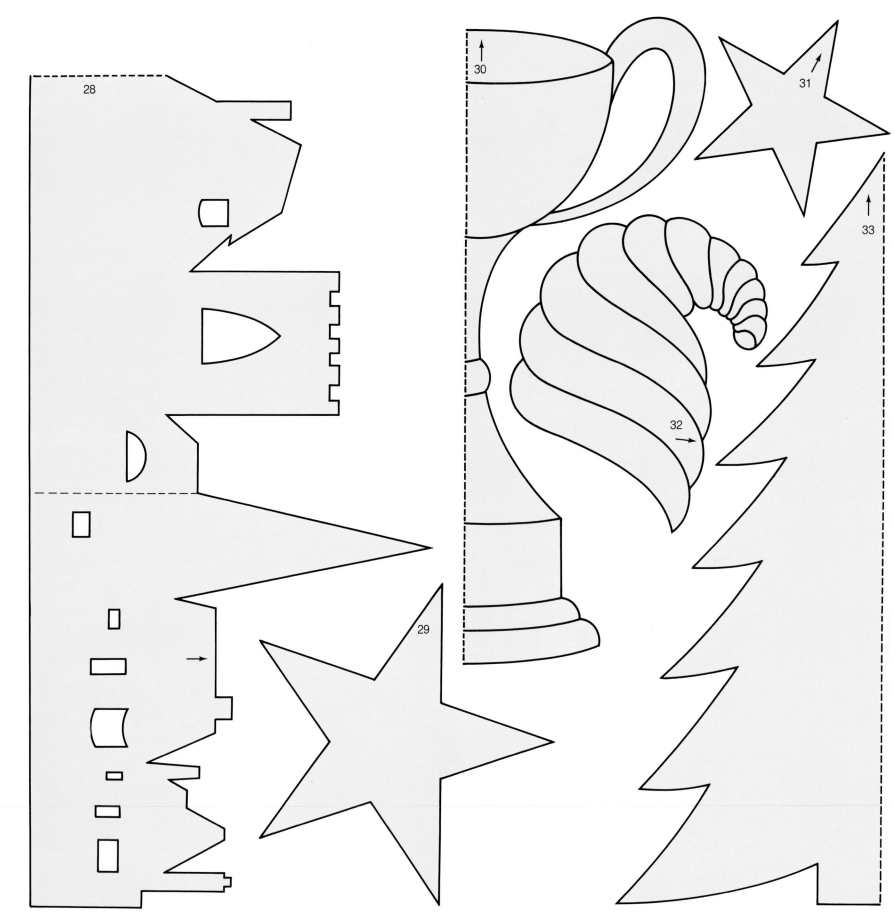

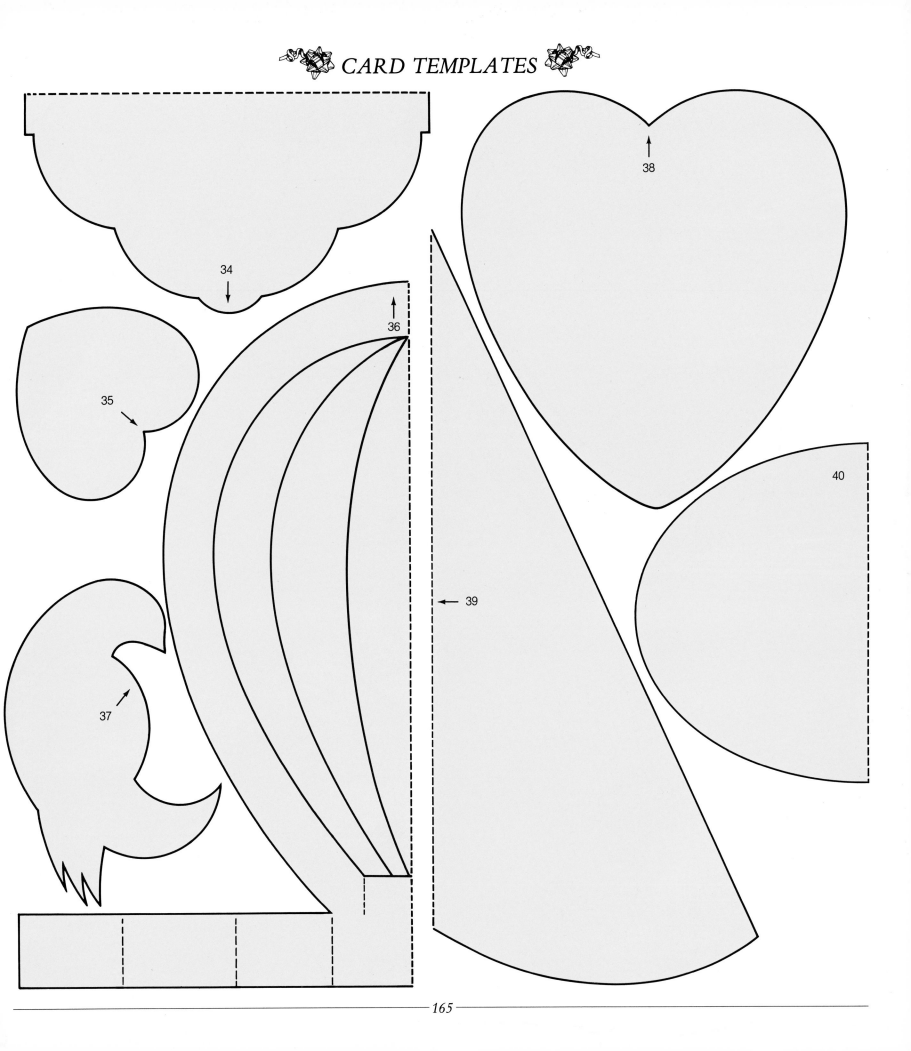

Needlepoint in Lilac (page 127)

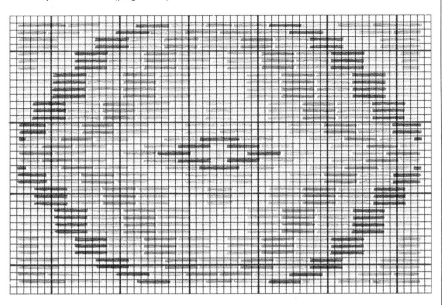

Tranquil Retirement (page 159)

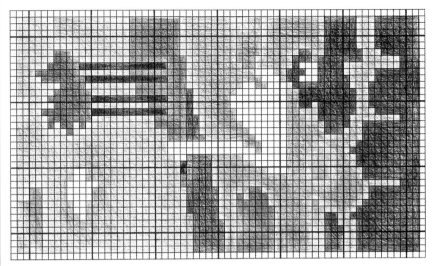

A Warm New Home Welcome (page 156)

Baby Girl in the Pink (page 157)

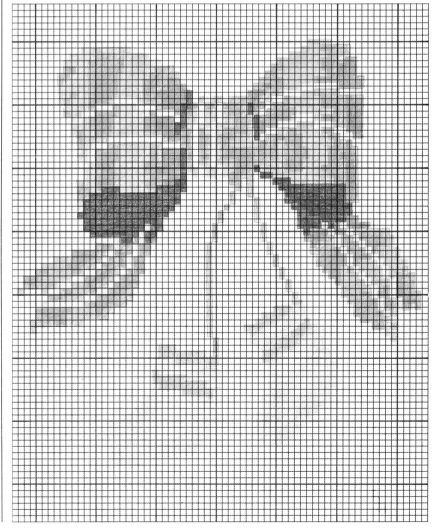

INDEX